play better tennis in 2 hours

Simplify the game and PLAY like THE PROS

OSCAR WEGNER
WITH Steven Ferry

McGraw Hill

Camden, Maine • New York
Chicago • San Francisco • Lisbon
London • Madrid • Mexico City
Milan • New Delhi • San Juan
Seoul • Singapore • Sydney • Toronto

The McGraw·Hill Companies

11 12 13 14 15 16 17 18 19 20 DOC DOC 1 5 4 3 2

ISBN: 978-0-07-143717-2
MHID: 0-07-143717-7

Library of Congress Cataloging-in-Publication Data
Wegner, Oscar
  Play better tennis in two hours : simplify the game and play like the pros /
Oscar Wegner with Steven Ferry.—1st ed.
       p.   cm.
Includes index.
  ISBN 0-07-143717-7
  1. Tennis. I. Ferry, Steven, 1953– II. Title.
  GV995.W42 2004
  796.342—dc22   2004020967

Questions regarding the content of this book should be addressed to
McGraw-Hill
P.O. Box 220
Camden, ME 04843

Questions regarding the ordering of this book should be addressed to
The McGraw-Hill Companies
Customer Service Department
P.O. Box 547
Blacklick, OH 43004
Retail customers: 1-800-262-4729
Bookstores: 1-800-722-4726

Photograph on page iii by Lucidio Studio Inc./Corbis.
Photographs by Steven Ferry unless otherwise noted.
Illustrations by Deirdre Newman.

contents

acknowledgments

I WOULD LIKE to thank these former top players for personally showing me the best of their game: Pancho Gonzalez, the serve; Pancho Segura, the two-handed forehand; Roy Emerson, the volleys; and Manuel Santana, the topspin forehand.

I would also like to thank Nina Bers, 1987 U.S. Junior Intercollegiate tennis champion, for her patient modeling for the photographs; Steven Ferry, for helping me write and photograph this book; and most of all, L. Ron Hubbard, who inspired my life with his works and insights into teaching and the nature of the human spirit.

introduction

IN THE 1960s, less than 10 million people played tennis in the United States. Then in 1968, professionals and amateurs were allowed to compete together for the first time in open tournaments, sparking an explosion of interest and TV exposure for the game. As a result, by the late 1970s, close to 40 million Americans were playing tennis.

However by the beginning of 2000, industry figures showed the number of players only ranged between 16 and 23 million, while official figures from the United States Tennis Association showed three times this number had left the game over the last twenty years.

Why did this happen?

As unpalatable as it may seem, the answer is from incorrect instruction—tennis had been taught one way, while the top pros played a completely different way.

That is until I ended my international playing days and began coaching at the Beverly Hills Tennis Club in California as an assistant to Pancho Segura, considered one of the greatest coaches ever. I soon realized that the most important details of the top pros' games were not only neglected but also actually violated by both conventional coaching and most entry-level teaching.

My own forehand stroke had been affected by poor coaching. Formerly a powerful, stinging weapon I had found on my own as a child, it was rendered inaccurate and ineffective during my tour-playing days after I was counseled to play "the proper way." Something was amiss.

Once I was free of the competitive pressures of the tennis tour, I discovered the answer to the riddle—tennis had been made too complicated. Simple. I then isolated the common denominators of the best strokes, and by establishing what was important to learn and what was not, I found that tennis was a game of hand-eye coordination only—not hand-eye-feet, as had been widely taught.

When focusing a player on hand movement only, I noticed the body coordinated itself naturally, resulting in the same fluid motions as the pros.

Just by following very simple but specific instructions on how to stroke the ball, and still focusing on the hand, players experienced an incredibly rapid rate of improvement. In the same way, you should expect to be a changed player after a couple of hours practicing this fundamental truth.

Beginners, when not overriding the motions they had acquired in learning to walk and run, found tennis to be an easy sport to learn. Beyond this, you, like all players, just need to determine the best way to handle the ball, maximizing your feel, power, and control—all of which the drills in this book make possible. This book will integrate the best techniques available with your own unique physique and develop your tennis based on your natural motor skills.

The Results

Encouraged by Pancho Segura, I first tested these fundamentals on a large following of Hollywood clientele, including Charlton Heston, Dinah Shore, and Dean Martin Jr. (whose tennis looked so good after his training that he was cast playing in the Wimbledon singles final against Guillermo Vilas in the movie "Players").

The Spanish Tennis Federation hired me in 1973 to coach the top juniors at the National Tennis School. I applied these same fundamentals, despite opposition from leading Spanish coaches, with astounding results. Within three months of my arrival, Spanish players using my techniques eliminated all the international competitors in the Monte Carlo Junior Tournament, resulting in four Spanish semifinalists. The coaches accepted the evidence and adopted my methods. From then on, Spain didn't have just a few winners—it had a crowd of them, an influx of new talent that continues to this day!

Returning to Florida in 1974, I opened my own tennis club, teaching those who were intrigued by my unorthodox but highly successful techniques.

In the 1980s, I was invited to Brazil, where I spent half that decade coaching in a small club and teaching local pros my coaching methods. Two juniors whom I coached went on to win the Junior Davis Cup in Miami for Brazil in 1993. Some years later, one of them, Gustavo "Guga" Kuerten, went on to win three French Open championships, and became World Champion in 2000 by beating Pete Sampras and Andre Agassi.

In 1990, I returned to the United States, where I wrote the forerunner to this book, *You Can Play Tennis in Two Hours*, and appeared weekly for four years on a nationally syndicated tennis show, *The New Tennis Magazine Show* (later called *Tennis Television*), on the Prime Network. An ambitious tennis father, Richard Williams, saw these shows and trained his young girls on my system for four years before sending them directly into the professional tennis circuit. A few years later, Venus and Serena Williams dominated the sport.

In 1994, I became a tennis commentator for ESPN Latin America, changing the entire continent's coaching ideas and methods. Starting in 1997, and for the next two years, ESPN International broadcast my tennis tips in English and Spanish to over 150 countries, initiating a coaching revolution around the world. Another tennis parent, this one in Thailand, had a youngster with the talent to become a pro, but very little tennis was being played in the country and even less coaching materials were available. When he saw the ESPN broadcasts, he ordered my videos to coach his son. Within a few years, Paradorn Srichaphan became one of the top players in the world.

The Russian Tennis Federation, which has worked with my first book since 1990, implemented my techniques in their junior programs, and the results are showing up in the professional ranks—a dozen Russian women are now ranked in the top one hundred of the world.

The Wegner Method

My system works for beginners as well as advanced club players and pros. It teaches the basics in a more natural way, hooking you on tennis forever. Because my system is easier to learn, you really can be playing better tennis in two hours.

What are the specific benefits you and other players may expect from the Wegner Method?

> Ease of movement on the tennis court
>
> Feeling you are well coordinated
>
> Excellent control of your shots
>
> No fear of missing the shot
>
> Ease of adjustment to difficult shots
>
> Ability to play without feeling rushed
>
> Certainty in your timing of the ball
>
> Constant improvement
>
> Gradual development of power
>
> Minimal amount of thinking
>
> Togetherness with the ball
>
> Ability to stay focused
>
> Knowing that you know a lot about the game
>
> Confidence in your skill

If you have ever been taught tennis before, look at the following table and note which teaching method best describes the way you play. When you have completed the book, review the list and see if anything has changed for you.

Before and After Assessment

TRADITIONAL COACHING	WEGNER METHOD
You have to prepare as fast as you can	Top professionals restrain themselves from reacting too quickly
Take your racquet back as soon as the ball leaves your opponent's racquet	The best pro players keep the racquet to their front until the ball is close
Start your stroke early	You have to wait for the ball

Before and After Assessment (cont.)

TRADITIONAL COACHING	WEGNER METHOD
Move forward on your serve	Pro players hit up on the serve, then fall forward
Put your left foot across to hit your forehand (closed stance)	Open-stance forehands are more powerful and natural
Keep your distance from the ball— usually an arm's length	Closer distances are better for power and control
Keep your arm straight on your forehand	Bending the arm on the forehand is much more natural
Step forward into the ball	Top pros emphasize lifting, not stepping in
Stay down through the stroke	It is more natural to pull up
Don't let your body lean back	The body does whatever is needed to make the shot
On your forehand, keep your racquet head above your wrist all of the time	All top pros drop the racquet head below the ball and below the hand and wrist at some point during their swing
You can hit the ball harder with a flat stroke than with topspin	You can hit the ball harder flat, but right out of the tennis court
Bend your knees only	Pro players bend whatever and wherever is natural
Move to the ball with side steps, then turn and hit	Pro players pivot and run to the ball
Make a ¼-turn grip rotation between forehand and backhand	No grip change is necessary for the two-handed backhand; for the one-handed backhand, pros bring the racquet parallel to the body to change grip, rather than focusing on rotating it
Finish your forehand pointing to your target	The arm comes across the body with the butt of the racquet usually pointing to the target at the end of the forehand stroke
Topspin is more stressful on your arm	Flat shots are harder on your arm
You have to hit deep all the time	The deeper you try to drive the ball during rallies, the more mistakes you'll make

Tennis is a wonderful adventure. After reading this book you'll love this sport more than ever, and your game will never be the same! In fact, I believe that as these techniques are adopted, tennis will regain and even surpass its earlier popularity.

How to Use This Book

This book has information for players of all levels. Some sections are very basic, written for beginners, while others are written for advanced players. These advanced sections are called "Play Like the Pros" (a full list is provided in the index). Beginners should skip these tips until they have completed the entire book. *Then* they may go back and read the advanced tips which will, undoubtedly, make more sense.

The book is set up so that you first study a section and then go onto a court and practice the specific drill for that section until you have mastered it. Only then should you move on to the next section.

The first chapter, Misconceptions, is targeted to people who have been exposed to the myths of conventional tennis teaching. *If you are a complete beginner, you should skip this section at first.* But if someone is trying to teach you concepts such as "get sideways," "take your racquet back early," "step into the ball," "hit through five balls in a row," or "follow through toward the target," you may need to review the Misconceptions chapter—and perhaps show it to your coach as well.

If you are an intermediate player, I recommend you read the whole book in order to isolate and adopt any new concepts to your game, practicing indicated drills as necessary.

Lastly, when you bump into a word that you do not understand fully, please do not guess what it means from the context—a bad habit being taught in many schools these days. Look it up in a dictionary and find the exact definition of the word being used.*

If you have any questions or difficulties concerning your own game, you can either log onto www.tennisteacher.com for more information or e-mail me at oscar@tennisteacher.com.

* Based on the technology of study developed by Mr. L. Ron Hubbard in the 1960s. For more information, visit www.appliedscholastics.org/learn_barr.php.

misconceptions

1

Serena Williams. [Art Seitz]

W H Y   I S   T E N N I S considered a difficult sport to learn and to improve upon? Mostly because of widely taught misconceptions that cripple a player's natural ability and make coordination as difficult as walking with several crutches at the same time.

Even many tennis professionals believe these misconceptions. But the test is, do they actually follow them when they play?

Observe and decide for yourself.

I have seen top players go into rapid decline in the later years of their career when adjusting to the conventional way. During their greatest years, of course, they were untouchable. Nobody could tell them to use any other technique but their own obviously successful style.

But soon after they felt some cracks in their armor they sought advice. "Flatten your strokes. You are getting older, you need more power," is one common culprit.

For most modern players, topspin strokes and ball rotation are great rungs on the ladder to success. At the top of their game, they can hit as hard as they want, sometimes flattening their strokes. But when their confidence wanes, the successful course of action is to rely on the safety of the topspin shots, without compromising the power or the margin for error.

Following are classic misconceptions that could impair your game. The top pros shown in this book are vivid examples of players who did not fall for these faulty ideas.

Myths versus Facts

MYTH: Learn every move—tennis is a game of positions, specific steps, and preparations that you must learn in detail.
FACT: Go to the ball in a natural, instinctive way, focusing only on what you do with the racquet and the ball.

In the mind of a tennis pro, a ground stroke is a channeled effort rather than thought. His eyes are focused on the ball. His "feel" is focused on what he does with the racquet, as its movement and angle determine his whole shot. He wants to feel the ball rather than think of the mechanics.

The player reaches in the proximity of the ball, finding it as if wanting to catch it. He thinks of nothing else but where he wants to send the ball, channeling all his effort into achieving this goal. His only mental image of position is the arm at the end of the swing, something he has related to his shot placement over the years.

His mental effort may be nothing more than to bring the arm and racquet to this "finish." At this point, this particular effort is over. He might keep the arm in this position for a short time, feeling the end of his swing and looking to see where the ball is going. However, his legs don't stay still. He may already be recovering from the shot or covering the court. But he has certainly related the end of his swing to where he wants his shot to land.

Most conventional teaching techniques have you relate the impact of the ball to the placement of your shot. This technique is excellent for your volleys. But on ground strokes, top pros focus on the finish of the swing, which is the main reason why they don't "choke," stopping their swing midway. The only part of the swing they know for sure is the finish. The rest of the stroke adjusts instinctively while finding the ball.

MYTH: Prepare as fast as you can.
FACT: Restrain yourself from reacting too quickly.

Although sometimes you have little time to swing at the ball, you must manage the time you have. With the ball at a medium or slow pace, a pro looks as if he isn't even trying.

So little is the effort required at this slower pace that many amateurs play great placement and control games seemingly without exerting themselves. They take their time to run and to stroke. They look terrifically coordinated. They don't look like pros, of course, because the speed of the ball is much slower, but they play like pros, managing time and effort efficiently.

Look at pros warming up or practicing, and you'll see how easily they move and how much time they have.

At high ball speeds, pros may look rushed, but there really isn't much upper body effort on their strokes prior to the hit. A pro finds the ball first, then explodes.

Of course, your legs have to move fast to enable you to intercept the ball. A good opponent will make you run, slide, bend, and jump. But while the legs move fast, the arms are waiting for the right moment to swing.

What is amazing about top pros is the separation between the body effort to reach the ball and the arm effort to strike it. They run for the ball first, trying to find it as if catching it, then they swing at it.

MYTH: Take your racquet back as soon as the ball leaves your opponent's racquet.
FACT: Keep your racquet to the front until the ball is close.

Conventional tennis teaching emphasizes taking the racquet back as

Roger Federer hitting forehand. [Art Seitz]

soon as you see the ball coming your way. The student is taught to make this preparation before starting to run, losing valuable time that should be used to reach the ball. Even at high ball speeds, this preparation should be made toward the end of the run.

Holding your racquet to the front keeps the racquet closer to the ball and helps you find it well. Although pros turn their shoulders, this is different from taking the arm back. Many top pros keep the nonplaying hand on the racquet during the first part of the flight of the ball to avoid taking the racquet back too soon. The ball bounces first, comes close to the player, then he swings at it.

Taking the racquet back early is probably the most common barrier to advancement taught in tennis today. The racquet is already in the forehand-ready position when holding it centered at your waist. The same holds true for the two-handed backhand, where grip changes are unnecessary.

Modern forehands and two-handed backhands are totally different from the old racquet-back technique. Instead of taking the racquet back right away, you "stalk" the ball with the racquet face, as if you were going to touch it. Then you hit. This stalking technique helps you find the ball. It also adjusts the backswing automatically to the speed and height of the ball and to the difficulty of the shot.

Don't commit your swing until after the ball bounces. You may approach the path of the ball from the moment it leaves your opponent's racquet. You may start to adjust your arms, but beware of committing your swing.

Taking your backswing early commits you to a swing path before you know exactly where the ball will be. Predicting exactly how the ball will bounce is not possible. Court surfaces are uneven in texture, and the ball will grab the ground differently depending on its speed and spin. If you start your ground stroke prior to the bounce, you may envision a perfect stroke, but you will have to adjust it to the bounce of the ball halfway through the forward swing.

This early backswing is the way most people were coached to play tennis throughout much of the sport's history. They started their swing, and then they adjusted as they were going through the ball. Only a few players excelled in adjusting to the ball before starting their swing, and they became the best players of their time.

At the high speeds of professional play there may not seem to be enough time to wait, but there is! Bear in mind that on hard courts

Justine Henin-Hardenne hitting forehand. [Art Seitz]

the ball slows down to 40 percent of its initial speed from baseline to baseline. A ball hit toward you from the other baseline at close to 50 mph will reach you at 20 mph.

Most pro players don't consciously know that they wait, but they do. It is an inner mechanism they developed in the early stages of their game.

If you were to ask a world-class player, "Do you take more time to return a second serve than a first serve?" the answer would be, "Of course I do." This shows that deep inside, the player waits for the right moment to stroke.

Here is a simple experiment that may convince some staunch supporters of the "racquet-back-early" technique that they should change their approach. Have another player serve to your forehand. Take your racquet back before he starts his service motion, and keep it there while he prepares to serve. When he serves, return from this backswing arm position. See how awkward it feels? I have done this experiment with some very good players, and it stiffened their returns. "Feels awful," I was told.

If you have ever wondered why so many beginners have trouble learning with the conventional racquet-back system, this is your answer. Good coordination means doing things at the proper time. In your ground strokes, learn to play the second curve of the ball; that is, the curve after the bounce.

Try this in practice. Start with slow, high-looping ground strokes. Choose your contact point before you take your racquet back for momentum. The contact point becomes apparent only after the bounce. On slow, high-looping balls, it occurs well after the bounce.

Can you picture waiting as long as possible before taking your racquet back? I know that this will be mentally difficult for those who have trained for years with the opposite method. You'll feel so late!

Starting your swing too early is a hard habit to break. But the player who waits for the right moment to swing will thrive. He'll find the ball so well—he'll feel it so much—when hitting either softly or at tremendous speeds.

MYTH: Hit the ball early.
FACT: Wait for the ball.

Hitting the ball early is a concept that needs to be debunked, even at the highest level of the game. I have seen too many players experience off days and not know exactly why.

It is one thing to advance on the court to cut your opponent's time or to hit on the rise, putting pressure on your opponent, but it is another thing to start the stroke earlier than needed.

Of course top players like to attack the ball, hitting it firmly, but at high ball speeds, even being two-hundredths of a second too early loses the magic. Errors keep creeping in, and the player doesn't understand what is happening. The "feel" is off.

For players who lift the ball with topspin, being slightly early makes it harder to lift. When facing a player with heavy topspin, being too early creates mis-hits. It may not be recognized as a mis-hit, but the response is weaker, less lively, and sometimes shorter.

A tennis ball is very lively. If you hit it straight on, it will bounce off your strings in less than a hundredth of a second. If, on the other hand, you approach the ball slowly with the racquet and then accelerate near the contact, you'll feel that the ball stays on your strings longer, then takes off.

Your may not be able to see it, but you will feel the difference if you hit a few balls this way.

The ball speed, even when applying the same amount of force, depends on how close to the contact point you start to apply your force. A bit too early, and you achieve plenty of power, but your control is gone.

If a pro persists in hitting earlier than usual—perhaps unaware that he is just a few hundredths of a second off that day, or that this particular court plays a shade slower than the one he practiced on—he starts losing his confidence. He starts tightening up. His feel is lessened and his touch is gone, and deep inside he is puzzled—"why?"

This problem is more likely to happen to players who relish earlier timing to achieve more ball speed. They are playing with fire, very close to the boundary of being too early. But on better days, the magic and the brilliance are there. They just seem to touch the ball and it shoots like lightning, streaking to the opponent's court.

The heavy topspin players, on the other hand, wait for the ball so much that it hurts. They have to muscle the ball much more than the earlier hitters to achieve the same ball speed; but regarding timing, they are in a safer zone. The chances of hitting too early are minimal. They would have to be off close to a tenth of a second, a fact more easily noticeable than the hundredths of a second that would throw off the early hitter.

If you find these concepts hard to grasp, go to a court. Toss the ball a little in front and to your side. Wait until after the bounce and use almost no backswing. Feel that you touch the ball before you hit it, then emphasize your follow-through. In the first few shots the ball may be going nowhere at all, but as you hit harder, you'll gradually realize how close to the ball you have to start accelerating to achieve both ball speed and maximum control.

You can observe that most of the top pros play this way. Most errors in pro tennis come from taking the arm back too soon or stroking too soon. You lose feel, you lose control.

This doesn't mean that you can't hit some balls early, or well in front, thus flattening your stroke. You just have to consider the risk factor involved. You may hit some great winners, but it may also cost you some points. The real risk is loss of topspin on the ball. This topspin, even if minimal, helps drop the ball into the court.

At higher speeds, the difference of one or two ball rotations between your hit and the landing of your shot may mean the difference of a foot or two in the length of your shot. The ball that used to drop just inside the line may go out. Repeated errors like this will erode a player's confidence, precipitating his decline.

It is better to strike farther back in relation to your body—achieving more topspin and control with plenty of power—than to seek the seemingly perfect winner that may cost you more points than it will win.

MYTH: Move forward on your serve.
FACT: Hit up on the serve, then fall forward.

Pushing forward with the body on the serve causes a tendency to hit down with the arm. Visually, it seems that you have to hit down to get speed on a serve. But the more you hit down, the more you have to open the racquet to hit the ball over the net, and the ball develops backspin instead of topspin, losing its downward curve.

At the high speeds played in professional tennis, the ball has to have some topspin, even in the hardest serves, both for accuracy and consistency. Top pros have been found to rotate their first serve above 3,000 rpm and second serves above 5,000 rpm. To produce this amount of rotation, your body needs to move up, and your arm must fully extend upward *past* the impact with the ball.

Most professionals hit upward on their serve, but sometimes it is not enough. I recall working with a young player at the beginning of his professional career. I had him stand on the service line, facing the back

Andy Roddick stretching up and leaning into his service motion. [Art Seitz]

fence with a bucket of balls. I gave him one instruction—"Hit the balls over the fence with some spin."

In the beginning he hit several balls into the fence and was slightly puzzled. He thought he was hitting up, but obviously it was not up enough. He continued until he hit every ball over the fence. Then we picked up the balls and he served normally. It took him a few minutes to adjust, but soon I saw a miracle. He had raised his serving to an incredible level of speed, depth, accuracy, and kick. He had all the talent. Once he understood the correct concept and feel, he could do no wrong.

This upward effort combined with hitting across the ball is even more pronounced on second serves. Hitting upward on the second serve instead of hitting forward helps place the ball into the service court with both speed and spin. As a result, you'll produce an "American Twist" serve, a pronounced topspin shot that will clear the net by a couple of feet or more and land in front of the service line. The ball may look slow at first, but it will kick fast and high.

Players who don't have this action either slow down their second serve or they risk a lot. A good American Twist server doesn't slow down the motion at all and feels plenty of power and confidence on the second serve.

MYTH: Put your left foot across to hit your forehand (closed stance).
FACT: Use an open stance for your forehand. It results in a more powerful and natural stroke.

An open stance is, quite simply, standing with both feet facing the net. Most formal lessons put students sideways to the net and have them step forward with the left foot.

However, the greatest forehands of modern times are definitely open-stance forehands. An open stance not only helps players stroke, but it also allows them to return more rapidly to the middle to cover the court. Also, while it is almost impossible to hit a good topspin forehand from a very closed stance, the opposite is true with a very open stance.

Hand-eye coordination, as it relates to tennis, is totally dependent on an athlete coordinating his hand movement with his visual perception of the motion of the ball. The rest of the body responds naturally and instinctively to the action of the hand without any mental effort on the part of the athlete.

As a simple analogy, visualize yourself reaching out to shake hands with an attractive Hollywood movie star while at the same time thinking about the position of your feet, whether your weight is on the front foot or the back one, and several other details. Would you even be able to find the star's hand?

Hand-eye coordination means precisely that: hand-eye, not hand-eye-foot-weight coordination. The Wegner Method is based on the simple revelation that to improve your hand-eye coordination, whether you are a beginner, an advanced player, or a pro, you only need to focus on the contact between the racquet and the ball.

This doesn't mean that players don't have favorite body positions in which they feel most comfortable, or balanced, or powerful. But they have identified those positions by feel, instinctively, not by words or mental commands.

MYTH: Keep your distance from the ball—usually an arm's length.
FACT: Move closer to the ball for greater power and better control.

How did you catch something thrown to you when you were young? Did you run as close to it as possible and then extend your arm to catch it, or did you try to keep your distance? You moved as close as possible. Most conventional tennis techniques teach you to keep your distance from the ball when hitting. However, advanced players and pros run to come close to the line of flight of the ball, then they slow down and hit the ball at their side.

MYTH: Keep your arm straight on your forehand.
FACT: Bend your arm on the forehand. It is a more natural movement.

On the forehand swing, bend your arm as if you were shaking hands. A bent arm makes it easier to adjust your distance to the ball. It also gives you more power because you are using your biceps, one of the strongest muscles in the body.

For a hard topspin shot, your racquet face needs to come over the ball to prevent the ball from sailing out. This is more easily done by bending the arm at the elbow, rather than keeping it straight.

MYTH: Step forward into the ball.
FACT: Emphasize lifting, not stepping forward.

Tennis is basically a vertical game. You are fighting gravity. You need the ball to clear the net, then drop into the court.

In your topspin strokes, you want more lift than forward power, both to clear the net and to rotate the ball. In the topspin forehand, there is a natural tendency to move forward with the right side of the

Serena Williams in an open stance as she slides into a shot. [Art Seitz]

body while pulling up. Likewise in the two-handed backhand, the left side tends to go forward. These are forceful upper body turns and lifting motions that put power into the shot.

Stepping forward or backward is a function of your adjustment to the ball. If the ball is short, you move in. If the ball is deep, you may move back.

MYTH: Stay down through the stroke.

FACT: Lift up through the stroke.

It is natural for your body to lift up during a swing. Lifting up helps accelerate the stroke or extend your reach.

In some situations, you may need to stay down to reach a ball, for example, if it is short or low. However, under normal circumstances, staying down may trap your swing rather than facilitate it. Top players develop a feel for the best position for a given shot, whether it is lifting up or staying down.

MYTH: Don't let your body lean back.

FACT: Let the body do whatever is needed to make the shot.

Many good players and professionals purposefully pull back their body to create more topspin. It adds to the safety factor of the shot, clearing the net and making the ball drop in the court.

In some shots, if you feel too close to the ball, pull back when you hit. This will give you a comfortable distance from the ball, good control, and added topspin rotation.

The arm feels lighter and more powerful when pulling up. You also feel that you have plenty of time during and after the stroke, and your racquet stays up a fraction longer at the end.

MYTH: Keep your racquet head above your wrist throughout your whole forehand swing.

FACT: Drop your racquet head below the ball and below your hand at some point in your forehand swing.

This fact is especially true on balls hit below waist level.

Even on high topspin shots, the racquet head sometimes drops below the hand. To hit from low to high, you obviously have to be below the ball at some point, and the most comfortable and effective way is to drop the racquet head sometime before impact. The more you drop, the more you can come up, and the more topspin you will have. The same goes for the two-handed backhand topspin stroke.

It doesn't matter whether you loop your stroke or go straight down and up. Just get below the ball and pull it up.

MYTH: You can hit the ball harder with a flat stroke than with topspin.

FACT: You can hit the ball harder with a flat stroke, but it will go right out of the tennis court!

Gustavo Kuerten following through high while pulling back. [Art Seitz]

A hard, flat ground stroke hit from net level or below, from anywhere inside your court, has no chance of landing inside your opponent's baseline—no matter how close to the top of the net you hit it—unless you hit the net, your opponent, or a bird.

With enough topspin, you can hit a 60 mph shot in the court with the same downward curve as a flat 40 mph shot.

Another consideration in hitting hard and flat is your chance of winning the point. Pros go for the percentage shots.

Let's say you are a pro, and you have a 50 percent chance of hitting a flat 50 mph ground stroke to a corner (if you're an advanced club player, you have maybe a 30 percent chance). What if your opponent hits it back somehow? Would you take another chance like that?

Match results are determined more by unforced errors than by great shots. At a professional level, unless the court is slick and fast, the ball keeps coming back and coming back. These players are both forceful and safe.

There is a perception that the game has changed in the last few years, with top pros seeking to finish the point from the baseline in a very forceful way. This held true for a few top players in earlier decades as well. Heavy topspin hitters like Tilden, Borg, and Lendl always relished finishing the point with a powerful shot while still preserving their safety with spin on the ball.

Today's powerful racquets have made this tactic easier. New equipment provides tremendous ball speed, and topspin players can hit hard winners while still focusing on landing the ball safely in the court.

If you want to kill the ball with a ground stroke, blast it with topspin and look like a tennis pro (or at least an approximation) rather than a baseball player.

MYTH: Bend your knees only.
FACT: Bend whatever or wherever is natural.

The instruction to bend only your knees combined with staying down through the stroke makes players look like broken puppets. Bend naturally—waist, knees, arms—looking like an athlete, not like a stiff marionette.

MYTH: Move to the ball with side steps, then turn and hit.
FACT: Pivot to run to the ball.

Stepping sideways to run to the ball is the most ridiculous teaching method I ever saw. It's another technique that makes players look like puppets. Players who are making good progress by playing naturally can have their coordination, timing, feel, and focus on finding the ball destroyed by a teacher who makes them sidestep first in moving to a distant ball.

Top players sometimes sidestep while they are waiting to see their opponent's next shot, or when the ball is right there and they want to keep their open stance. But to purposely sidestep to run to a distant ball is crazy.

Nothing is more natural, graceful, and efficient than turning toward wherever you are going, leaning in that direction, and taking a few steps, gently and nonchalantly. Roger Federer, one of the greatest pros ever, plays this way. He looks smooth and fast, but all he does is lean and turn perfectly in the direction he wants to go. He seems to have ages to reach the ball. He isn't the quickest, he just has the most natural moves.

MYTH: Make a ¼-turn grip rotation between the forehand and backhand.
FACT: Do not change your grip for the two-handed backhand. Just add the left hand with its own forehand grip. For the one-handed backhand, bring your racquet parallel to your body to change your grip, rather than just focusing on rotating it.

If you have a two-handed backhand, you don't need to rotate the grip at all. The right hand can keep the forehand grip, while the left hand does most of the work throughout the stroke.

If your backhand is one-handed, the technique is different. You need to change your forehand grip to a backhand grip to have better racquet support at impact. Move your racquet to a position parallel to the front of your body, turning to your left, while the grip slides inside your right hand, changing position.

This change occurs primarily in the bottom portion of the hand, closest to the little finger. The fingers go from a spread-out position on the forehand grip to a close-together position for the backhand grip.

The palm of your hand is now on the top portion of the racquet grip to achieve a more perpendicular position of the arm to the racquet. This gives you much better support while hitting topspins, too. You can go to the extent of placing your thumb in the back bevel of your racquet handle.

You can test this grip by pressing the racquet flat against a wall or a tennis court fence, as if you were contacting the ball with your backhand. If your grip is OK, you'll feel plenty of support for your push.

For the one-handed backhand slice, the grip change from forehand to backhand is smaller, and the fingers remain spread apart. Here a ⅙-turn in grip rotation is more accurate, but this change is always larger toward the little finger than toward the index finger.

No matter what grip change you need, feel your grip, rather than looking at it. Looking at your grip and constantly worrying over it being correct takes valuable attention away from finding the ball.

MYTH: Point your racquet toward your target at the end of the forehand stroke.
FACT: Bring your racquet across your body toward your left shoulder to finish your stroke.

Pointing the racquet toward the target makes for a straight arm forehand. However bending your arm up toward your left shoulder will give you several advantages. You'll have more power, control, and topspin and be better able to close the racquet face angle. You'll have better balance and momentum to turn back toward the center of the court after your shot. And you'll prevent undue stress on your arm.

The same is true for the two-handed backhand. Bend both arms toward your right shoulder to achieve a full topspin swing.

In the one-handed backhand, the right arm will finish pointing approximately to the target or to the right of it, whether it is a topspin shot, where the arm finishes high, or a slice, where the arm finishes low. However the wrist never "breaks" to have the racquet point in that direction. The racquet will end up at an angle approximately perpendicular to the arm, whether the racquet moves over (topspin) or under (slice) the ball.

MYTH: Topspin is more stressful for your arm.
FACT: Flat shots are harder on your arm.

Although topspin requires more physical effort overall than conventional tennis, it distributes the stress impact over a wider area.

A ball coming at you and met squarely ("flat" in tennis jargon) puts the stress on your arm and tends to turn your racquet. You need to tighten your grip substantially, as well as your arm and shoulder, to put force into your swing.

Because of gravity, which affects your body as well as the ball, some of the impact force is dissipated through your body and pushes you toward the ground. On flat shots, this gives the feeling that your feet are firmly planted on the ground.

The topspin shot, on the other hand, is an upward movement. Your

Andre Agassi has both feet well off the ground as he hits a big forehand. [Art Seitz]

force is actually counteracting gravity. You feel light on your feet, sometimes coming off the ground. The force of the incoming ball is dissipated or canceled by your upward force. It may tend to ground you, but since you are pulling up anyway, you don't feel it as much as in the flat strokes.

This lift may save your lower and knees back from torsion stress. Of course you have to bend down, then pull up in your topspin shots. Sometimes you may jump, even while on the run. But these movements are truly natural, nothing that humans haven't done for millions of years.

With topspin, the stress on the arm is also diminished by the fact that some of the impact is dissipated into spin. The incoming ball travels downward on your racquet strings while you are pulling up. Topspin hitters usually contact the ball below the center of the strings, helping keep the racquet closed. Flat hitters tend to hit either on the center of the strings or above it.

Hitting below the center, you can hit a hard topspin shot without having to lock up on the racquet with your hand. The racquet path isn't disturbed much even if your grip is quite loose.

On the contrary, you need to tighten your grip with a flat shot, or your racquet may fly in a direction other than your shot. You counter those forces by tightening your hand and arm and planting your feet firmly on the ground.

In a very graphic way, hitting hard topspin shots feels like taking off in an airplane. By comparison, hitting forceful flat shots feels like crashing to the ground.

MYTH: You have to hit deep all the time.
FACT: The deeper you try to drive the ball during rallies, the more mistakes you'll make.

Unless you are hitting an approach shot (moving toward the net as you hit), where a deep shot is desired to force your opponent back, your goal is to keep the ball well inside the court.

If you constantly strive for depth, you play a high-risk game. The ball may travel much deeper than intended, overshooting your opponent's baseline.

Over 80 percent of the ground strokes at the top professional level bounce closer to the service line than the baseline. In a rally, just clearing the service line is enough depth. Then if the ball goes deeper, it will still land in the court.

I have seen top players start a match without much confidence, but coolly and safely keep the ball in play with plenty of topspin, mixed

Maria Sharapova getting under the ball to lift it up and over. [Art Seitz]

with a few sliced backhands, nothing too close to the lines. They work themselves into the match, grinding their way into their opponent's resistance. Then, as the match progresses, perhaps with a set under their belt, they steamroll their opponent, hitting powerfully all over the court. Wonderful, wonderful topspin, so powerful yet so safe!

Bjorn Borg won innumerable matches and championships doing just that on his ground strokes, hitting the ball with more topspin than anyone of his time.

Roger Federer is another of the great topspin players of all time. Depth is not critical for him, but his power drives a high percentage of his shots deep.

Federer is the most complete player of the current generation and perhaps the most exciting to watch. He can switch from safety to power or to touch shots in the blink of an eye. Sometimes he elects to tough it out from the baseline. Other times he storms the net right from the start of the point. He is undoubtedly a perfect example of the modern game: tremendous power tamed with topspin.

The success of these great players obviously depends on their mixture of power and control. With the newly developed wide-body racquets, hitting the ball flat at high speeds makes for more errors. A backspin on your volleys, even if minimal, will add to your control and feel of the ball.

From the backcourt, do the opposite and roll the ball up. The more topspin, no matter how hard you hit, the sooner the ball will drop.

If you want to hit the ball deeper in a rally, hit it harder or higher. Hit it with enough topspin, and it will land in front of your opponent's baseline and jump. You'll be risking less than if you flatten out your shots for more depth. With topspin, your shots will be harder for your opponent to return.

In Conclusion

Take a new, fresh look at the pros. Instead of watching the ball travel back and forth, fix your eyes on the player of your choice. Watch his moves—how he prepares, when he starts to stroke, how he hits the ball, how he follows through and finishes, the way he returns to the middle, and most importantly, how he finds the ball.

Top players are all good athletes, but they are not superhuman. Their technique is obviously the most important factor contributing to their success. Therefore, there is no reason to teach a beginner or an advanced student in opposition to how the top pros play and claim that it is the right way to learn the game. On the contrary, using the same basic principles as the top pros speeds the learning process, is more relaxing, and helps make the game more enjoyable. And that is what the Wegner Method is all about.

basic tools and rules 2

EVER SINCE the first tennis games were played on a grass court in England during the late nineteenth century, the sport of tennis has intrigued sports enthusiasts around the world. Today tennis is highly organized. Competitions range from club tournaments to local leagues and from state and national tournaments to professional championships, such as the four famous Grand Slams: Wimbledon, the U.S. Open, the French Open, and the Australian Open.

Switzerland's Roger Federer, 2003 and 2004 Wimbledon champion, serves to American Andy Roddick during the semifinals at Wimbledon's famous Centre Court. The first Open tournament was held at Wimbledon in 1968. [Art Seitz]

Equipment

THE RACQUET

Tennis is a game that combines *power* and *feel*. If you have a powerful body and an aggressive game, choose a stiff racquet and tight strings. If you prefer to play with finesse rather than force, choose a flexible racquet with moderate tension.

The area in the middle of the strings is called the *sweet spot* because it's the most responsive when hitting the ball. Flexible racquets have a larger sweet spot. Each brand is unique in terms of how large the sweet spot is. The idea that you have to hit the ball with the center of the racquet is an old one. In modern racquets, especially those strung with high-tech, thinner strings, the area of good response extends almost to the frame. In fact, hitting the ball about halfway between the center of the strings and the edge of the frame makes the racquet feel most stable.

Racquet Sizes

Racquets come in an ever-increasing variety of sizes, shapes, and materials, which can make choosing one a puzzle. Modern racquets can be as light as 8 ounces, with the average around 10 to 12 ounces. The maxi-

The word **racquet** originally comes from the Arabic word **rāhah**, and more recently from the Middle French word **raquette**, both meaning **palm of the hand**, and for good reason—tennis was once played with the hand. Although the game is now played with a racquet, it is still useful to think of your racquet as an extension of your hand.

The parts of a tennis racquet.

Shorter racquets with proportionally larger heads help teach children and build their confidence.

mum length is 29 inches. The maximum string area for tournament play cannot be more than 15½ inches long by 11½ inches wide. Adult grip sizes start at 4⅛ inches around the handle, then 4¼, 4⅜, 4½, and up.

The most popular racquets for non-pro adults are those with larger heads, up to 110 (which refers to the string area in square inches) and weighing about 10 to 11 ounces. Top pros tend to use midsize racquets, up to 107 square inches. Racquets with large heads and small, comfortable grip sizes fitted to the size of the hand are easiest for most players. Overall, choose the racquet that feels best when holding it comfortably loose. If you can, try out several before buying one, and test-play those that feel best. Each brand has a surprisingly different feel.

Choking Up on the Racquet

For some children and adults, it's easier to start playing tennis by *choking up* on the racquet, which is holding the racquet between the throat and the grip. This position makes it easier for a person new to the sport to control the ball. Also there is less of a tendency to swat at the ball. As soon as you're hitting successfully, gradually slide your hand down the handle until you reach the normal grip position described in Chapter 4, The Forehand.

Some people like to start with the hand closer to the throat of the racquet, others midway, and others directly on the racquet grip. Vary the

GRIP SIZE

Grip sizes generally start at a circumference of 4⅛ inches, increasing to 4¼, 4⅜, 4½, 4⅝, and 4¾. These are usually called grip sizes 1, 2, 3, 4, 5, and 6, respectively. The consensus within the industry is that the grip must be large enough to leave a space between the tip of the middle finger and the thumb pad that is the width of the player's index finger.

I find this rule counterproductive, especially with the modern, efficient techniques described in this book. With such grip sizes, a player needs to increase the tightness of his grip considerably to control the racquet. A smaller grip size, which allows the tip of the middle finger to be close to the thumb pad, enables the player to keep a looser grip on the racquet, resulting in a better feel of its position. Furthermore, smaller grip sizes make it easier to play at net, while larger grips make net play cumbersome. Lastly, smaller grip sizes allow slight changes of grip to become automatic, making racquets, especially lighter-weight models, feel like magnificent magic wands.

I have a very large hand. Back in the days when I was on tour, I used a large-grip (4¾ inches) wooden racquet, which resulted in plenty of elbow trouble. Thanks to the development of larger racquet heads, which are fairly flexible, and the use of a smaller grip size (4¼ inches), I no longer suffer from tennis elbow, even when playing for as long as four hours. And I enjoy a greater feel for the ball. •

RACQUETS AND STRING TENSION

Both the ball and strings deform on impact. Looser strings deform more and for a longer period of time than tight strings. Therefore, string tension affects the response of the racquet. Furthermore, strings of different brands may have widely differing responses, based on their composition and thickness.

Strings are made of nylon, polyester, Kevlar, or natural gut from cow intestines. Natural gut is the most responsive string but the shortest lasting. String thickness, called **gauge**, is measured around the circumference. Gauges range from 1/15 of an inch (15-gauge) at the thickest to 1/19 (19-gauge) at the thinnest, which is the most responsive. The convention of using "L" after a gauge number signifies a half measure. For example, 16L means a circumference of 1/16.5 inches.

Racquet frames have widely differing responses among brands and models based on the size of the head and the frame material. These differences result in varying degrees of flexibility. Sizes range from approximately 90 square inches of string bed to about 110 square inches—the larger the head, the more flexible the racquet. For decades, manufacturers pushed stiffer racquets, which were a one-shot solution to a lack of technical skill. With the techniques in this book, you'll develop the skills to use the most flexible and responsive racquet.

String tension plays an important role in both the power and feel of your game. While lower string tension may seem to create more ball velocity—power—this is not necessarily true. A player may use twice the muscular force yet not achieve twice the ball speed. The strings, deformed by the impact, may start to return to their original shape while still compressing the ball, making it seem as if the ball is sticking to the string bed, and affecting the speed of the ball. This phenomenon differs with string type and tension and also whether a player is hitting the ball dead center or toward the side of the string bed (the preferred choice for top pros). The player may not realize why two apparently equal swings produce quite different ball speed results and therefore placement.

How do top players choose their racquets? Easily—by feel. They try a racquet, and either it feels good or it doesn't. The same goes for string tension. If the racquet feels fairly good, the pro may try it at a slightly different string tension. If the racquet feels too light, he may put a small strip of lead tape on the frame at different locations to increase its weight.

With this wide range of variables, the easiest choice—and my recommendation for a racquet—is a large-framed racquet strung with 17-gauge, synthetic gut (16-gauge is too thick, 18-gauge breaks too much).

If you are a touch player, without a big swing, string the racquet at the low end of the recommended tension. I use 17-gauge, synthetic-gut string strung at 50 pounds of tension on the main strings and 52 pounds on the cross strings. When strung like this the result is 52 pounds overall, as the cross strings tighten the already strung main strings.

If you are a hard hitter, stick with the 17-gauge string, but the string tension should be closer to the higher end of the recommended tension for your frame, such as 60 pounds on the main strings and 62 pounds on the cross strings.

If you are an average power hitter with a long swing or a big topspin player, go halfway between the recommended high- and low-end tensions.

What do some of the top pros use?

Professional players tend to change the string tension in response to the court surface and type of ball being used in a tournament. These players have professional stringers who string their racquets at the tension they request for each venue. ●

Choking up on the racquet.

position of your hand until you find a position that's comfortable for you and gives you the most control. After a few tries, you will know what feels best at your current stage. Some players go through all the drills gripping the racquet by choking up. This is perfectly all right, too. You'll build confidence as you progress, so follow your instincts.

THE BALL

Competition tennis balls are yellow, weigh about 2 ounces, and have a diameter between 2.5 and 2.875 inches. Slight variations in size and

Foam training balls are useful because they don't hurt if they hit you, and they allow you to practice at home without damaging the furniture.

weight are allowed in tournament play, even the Grand Slams, but all balls must have specific bounce characteristics.

Tennis balls are designed either for hard courts with an asphalt or cement base, or for softer indoor and outdoor clay courts. You can use larger—3.5 inches—training balls made of foam, which bounce like a regular ball but are extremely light. I have found regular clay-court balls much easier on the arm, although they do not last as long as hard-court balls. Pressureless balls are made of harder rubber and are harder on the arm.

THE COURT

Originally, in the 1800s, the tennis court was designed only for *singles* play, where one person played against another. Players later added an area 4½ feet wide along each side of the court to make it competitive and roomy enough for two people playing on each side of the net (called *doubles*). For singles, use the inside lines down the edges of the court, called the *singles lines*. They create a playing area 27 feet wide and 78 feet long. For doubles, use the outer sidelines, or the *doubles lines*, for a wider playing area.

The net is 3½ feet high at the net posts. To keep the net taut, a vertical strap pulls down on the net in the center, bringing it to the regulation height of 3 feet.

The word **court** was first used by Italians two thousand years ago when they said **cortem** to refer to an enclosed area.

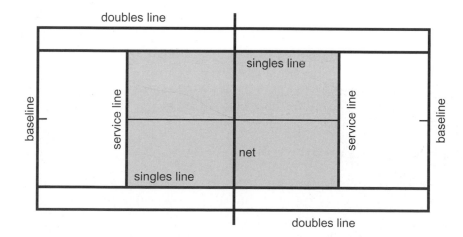

The lines establish boundaries for singles and doubles play and mark the service line *(the maximum depth of the serve) and the* baseline *(the maximum depth of all other shots). If the ball bounces beyond a* boundary line, *it's out of play. If it touches the line, it's considered* good—*to have landed within that area.*

The Game of Tennis

The purpose of the game is to hit the ball over the net so your shot lands in your opponent's side of the court, within the sidelines and baseline. When your opponent can't hit the ball back into your court within one bounce, you win the point.

A fundamental part of the game that many beginners do not realize is keeping the ball *in play*—continuing to hit the ball so it falls safely within the court. In my international coaching experience, I've noticed that Americans, perhaps influenced by baseball, focus too much on hitting the ball hard. The best way to play, especially in the beginning stages, is to be patient and in control of the ball. Not only will more people want to practice and play with you, but you'll be able to exercise more and ultimately win more games.

When your opponent hits the ball to you, it will:

1. Hit the net and stay on your opponent's side of the court (you win the point)
2. Land outside the sidelines or the baseline (your point again)
3. Come over the net and bounce within the lines on your side (the ball is still in play)

At this point, it is your job to return the ball (hit it back).

4. If you hit the ball after it bounces, it's called a *ground stroke*, because you stroked (or hit) the ball after it bounced once on the ground
5. If you hit the ball in midair before it bounces, it is called a *volley*
6. If you hit the ball into the net, out-of-bounds, or after it has bounced a second time, you lose the point

GETTING STARTED

Be sure to manage your time on the court. If you're a beginner, overdoing your first lessons can result in physical or mental burnout. I suggest spending a maximum of one hour on the court your first day. For some young children and less fit adults, twenty to thirty minutes is plenty. When you return to the court the next day, go over what you learned the first day before proceeding.

On the diagram below, use your fingertip as a tennis ball and go through each of the six possible outcomes until you have them firmly in mind:

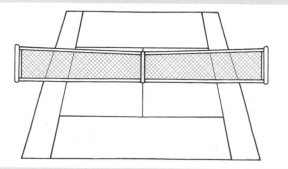

- your opponent's ball hits the net
- your opponent hits the ball out-of-bounds
- your opponent hits a good shot

and

- you return the ball with a ground stroke
- you return with a volley
- you lose the point by hitting the ball into the net, out-of-bounds, or after it bounces twice ●

Each student has a different learning speed. Continue a drill until you are hitting the ball where you want and have a good feel for the swing. Do each drill until you can repeat the swing each time and achieve roughly the same results.

During the early days of playing tennis you build habits that last a lifetime. Focus on the simple techniques here and don't do anything else, no matter how good and "knowledgeable" somebody else's suggestions may seem. Many people who are generous with their advice are not really familiar with teaching tennis in a natural way, no matter how well they play themselves. They may pass on faulty ideas they learned from conventional tennis teaching, and these ideas may impede your progress. With the Wegner Method, you can learn in hours what usually takes months to master. But if you mix in additional or contradictory advice, your focus may change, eventually lessening your feel for the ball.

Volley was first used by the Italians several thousand years ago when they would say **volare** to communicate the idea of flying. Today, in tennis, we use **volley** to mean hitting the ball on the fly.

CHOOSING A GOOD TEACHER

Choosing a good teacher, the right teacher, may mean the difference between loving tennis and hating it. There are several traits you should look for when choosing your teacher.

- A good teacher spends time assessing a student's skills, such as hand-eye coordination and balance. The teacher starts students at the lowest level, coaxing them to play so as to evaluate their hand-eye coordination. A few balls tossed to the student, some bouncing high, some low, some close, some far away, will give the teacher a good idea of the student's abilities. If any of the students have talent, the teacher can move them along faster so as not to bore them if they learn the drills quickly or already have the skills.
- A good teacher adjusts the speed of the learning experience to a student's physical and mental abilities. The teacher introduces new drills at the student's pace, allowing her to practice each drill until she totally understands it and is confident and comfortable. Only then does he move the student on to a more difficult drill.

    For example, your teacher may have you practice a particular stroke without the ball until your muscles become used to the natural movement and flow. Then he will feed you the ball gently, perhaps having you just catch it until you can do so proficiently. Then he may progress the lesson by throwing the ball to you so you can hit it with the stroke you've just practiced. And so on, always making it easy so you win all the way.
- A good teacher has plenty of patience, awareness, and understanding. It takes all of these qualities to assess and develop a student's ability while also building up his or her confidence.

    Even if you are severely impaired in your sense of movement and spatial orientation, a good teacher showing patience and understanding and relaying correct techniques will have you loving tennis for the rest of your life.

Group lessons usually fail to have a 100 percent success rate because the teacher is not adjusting to individual students and may move to the next drill while some students are still having difficulty with the previous one. If this happens to you, you may be better off taking private lessons. Also, sometimes a group is not harmonious, in which case the teacher should divide the group into smaller groups of equal ability.

I have taught people successfully who told me they were totally uncoordinated. Using patience and diligence, I found each student's absorption rate for new information and, detail by detail, I built their coordination first and then their game.

Within as short a time as one hour, they were different people, confident that they could perform. So I know this approach to teaching works.

When teaching a group, I often pair up students so the better player brings the lesser one up. Instant empowerment—now the better student becomes a coach! This approach is something you could ask your teacher to adopt, too.

Tennis is easy to learn and easy to teach. By applying the principles of the Wegner Method, there will be no failures. Everyone learns, everyone improves. Why? Because this method is the natural way to play and the most efficient way to use muscles. Right from the start, everyone plays in his or her own way, expressing his or her own feel and preference.

These principles, laid down at the beginning, make your foundation, feel, and coordination very strong. You provide the talent, and these techniques will do the rest. •

IT'S EASIER THAN YOU THINK

For close to a century, tennis has been considered a difficult sport to learn. You are encouraged to be mindful of where to place your arms and feet and to watch your balance, weight transfer, footwork, swing, and more. Tennis teacher associations have cultivated the belief that you can't play like the pros. Both these premises are false, and yet are still in vogue around the world.

The truth is that tennis is a simple game and easy to learn. Just watch the top players to see how naturally and fluidly they play—a style that you too can achieve.

At such a high level of play, of course, pros make great efforts both to reach a distant ball and to add speed to their shots. But, in terms of attention, you should concentrate solely on finding the ball well and playing it back with the racquet as if you were playing it with your hand. Pro players don't worry about body position; they just balance themselves while trying to optimize their strokes, whether they are standing or on the run chasing the ball. They basically want the hand near the ball, so they can find the ball better with the racquet and make it easier to hit it as hard as they want.

You can learn this focus quickly if you simplify things. Practice hitting balls while you walk forward, backward, and to each side of the court, without any attention on your feet, just as if you were simply walking in your kitchen or jogging in the park. This teaches you an independence of the arms and hands from the rest of your body, so you can control your shots even with the body extended and the legs pumping fast.

Over time, your body will learn how to help the stroke. You'll feel natural, balanced, safe, and increasingly powerful, but always in control. •

strokes

Roger Federer. [Art Seitz]

Flow and Natural Strokes

TENNIS IS a flowing game, a game of your to-getherness with the ball. While the ball is in play, think of nothing—just observe, run, feel, and control the ball. Your racquet is an extension of your hand. The rest of your body accompanies the hand naturally, so you don't have to worry about coordination or footwork. You probably learned to move like that years ago, when you learned to walk, to run, or to catch something falling or thrown to you.

Nobody needs to tell you now that your right foot takes one step, then your left foot takes one step, and so on. Nobody should even make you think of that, changing your focus from controlling the ball or distracting your attention with things you do naturally anyway.

THE FOREHAND

Assuming you are right-handed, when you hit a ball to the right side of your body, it is called a *forehand* shot because the *fore* or front part of your right hand is leading the shot. For more, see Chapter 4, The Forehand.

Forehand: the palm of the hand is facing the ball.

THE BACKHAND

When you stroke a ball coming in on your left side, it is called a *back-hand* shot because the stroke is led with the *back* side of your right hand.

The Two-Handed Backhand

Some people use both hands to hold the racquet when hitting a back-hand. For this stroke, the left hand drives the power, with the right hand still in the forehand position.

For more, see Chapter 5, The Backhand.

THE VOLLEY

When you move up to the net and hit the ball before it bounces on your side of the court, it is referred to as a *volley*. When you hit the ball on your right before it hits the ground, it is called a *forehand volley*.

When you hit the ball to your left before it hits the ground, it is called a *backhand volley*. See the photos opposite.

For more, see Chapter 8, The Volley.

Ground strokes—the forehand and back-hand—are hit after the ball has bounced once in your court. **Volleys** are hit in the air before the bounce. The word **shot** describes the fact that you have hit a tennis ball with a racquet. It comes from English spoken 1,500 years ago, when **ge-sceot** referred to an implement used for shooting.

Strike, **stroke**, and **hit** all describe the **action** of hitting the ball. Think of **stroking** the ball rather than striking it, to increase your feel of the racquet brushing the ball.

Backhand: the back of the hand is facing the ball (left).

With two hands on the rac-quet, it is still called a back-hand. The left hand drives the power, with the right hand more relaxed than the left (right).

THE OVERHEAD

The ball may be coming at you high above your head in what is called a *lob*. In this case, when you hit down on the ball, it is called an *overhead* or *smash* (see right photo below). The smash can be taken *on the fly* (before it hits the ground) or after the ball has bounced well above your head. For more, see Chapter 9, The Lob and Smash.

Forehand volley (top left).

Backhand volley (bottom left).

The overhead, or smash, is hitting a ball coming to you high above your head.

WHAT IF I'M LEFT-HANDED?

For those of you who are left-handed, you use a forehand shot when the ball comes to the left side of your body (because the fore—front—part of your left hand is leading the shot) and a backhand shot for a ball that comes to your right (because the stroke is led with the back side of your left hand).

Throughout the book, you'll find instruction on strokes, grips, and shots detailed for right-handers. You'll also find key strokes explained and illustrated for left-handers. For all other coaching, left-handers can reverse the left-right directions. ●

A left-hander's forehand (left).

A left-hander's one-handed backhand (right).

A left-hander's two-handed backhand.

Racquet Angle

A fundamental rule for any stroke is that the angle of the racquet face determines almost exclusively the direction in which the ball goes when you hit it. The finer points in your game will come as you realize that you are basically playing tennis with your hand, not the racquet. The angle of your hand is, in effect, the angle of your racquet. For top pros, the hand and the racquet are synonymous.

Conventional teachers tell players to place their body and feet in certain precise positions to hit the ball to a certain spot. They even tell players to follow the path of the ball with the racquet for a certain period of time during the swing to ensure the ball flies in that direction.

This is all too complex and unnecessary, and you can prove it to yourself. If you sit on a chair on the court, you will still be able to hit the ball to the right corner of the court while moving your racquet to the left. How? Because you just have to angle your racquet face to the right. The direction of the ball depends on the angle of the racquet.

The same principle applies for how high or low the ball flies when you hit it. Open the racquet by rotating your forearm to bring the top edge back (don't change your grip), and the ball flies higher than if you hold the racquet perpendicular to the ground. Close the racquet angle (top edge forward), and the ball goes lower.

In the early stages of learning, angle your hand and racquet slightly

Angle the racquet face toward the right side of the court to send the ball there (left).

Angle the racquet face to the left, and the ball goes left (right).

Use your hand to mimic a few swings for each of the following:

1. Forehand
2. Backhand with one hand and two hands
3. Forehand volley
4. Backhand volley with one hand
5. Overhead ●

Open the racquet face to send the ball higher (left).

Close the racquet face to send the ball lower (right).

upward. As you become more proficient, it becomes second nature to swing upward and across the body. You'll notice the racquet face will be almost vertical to the ground, not angled open or closed. As you practice, you will find that small angles can make a big difference. The top pros hit the ball upward so forcefully for topspin that they need to keep the racquet face relatively closed so the ball does not sail out of the court. Obviously, if you close the racquet too much, the ball won't clear the net.

THE SERVE

The first hit in any game is called a *service* or *serve*. When you serve, stand behind the baseline to one side. Look over the net and notice the line down the middle of the court. This is called the *centerline*. The

Standing on one side of the court, serve across the net diagonally to land the ball inside your opponent's service court (left).

Move naturally to the ball to return the service, whether it comes to your forehand or backhand (right).

line that cuts across the court on your opponent's side is called the *service line*. To serve, you have to hit the ball over the net diagonally to land in the box marked by the centerline and service line. The person receiving the ball stands near the baseline, adjusting his position to best return the serve after the ball has bounced. For more, see Chapter 6, The Serve.

3. MASTER THE SERVE, LESSON ONE

On the diagram below, use your finger to trace the trajectory of the ball and its bounce in the service court from both sides of the baseline. •

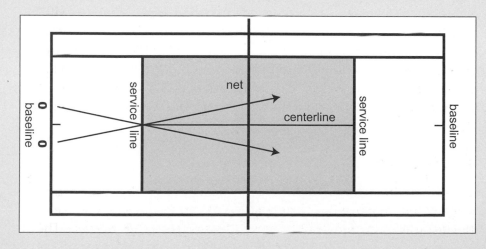

You serve one point from the right, the next point from the left, and so on.

DYNAMICS VERSUS MECHANICS

In tennis, you can think of **dynamics** as the variations in force and intensity in a player's performance. **Force** is the velocity the player imparts to the ball. **Intensity** is the constant determination of the player to move diagonally across the court or forward to intercept the ball's path and thus cut the opponent's time to recover from the shot just made. **Mechanics** are the different physical components—and muscular contractions or elongations—that make up a stroke.

Many advanced players see these as the same thing. They don't focus on the mechanics and instead play dynamically. They go after the ball, and all they do is decide when, how hard, and where they are going to hit it. They know they're applying correct mechanics at a deep level, without even thinking. Just like a concert pianist, they focus on the feel, not the "how to." Other players focus on the mechanics and don't feel as decisive and natural.

What's the optimum way to play?

By far the number one factor is having correct, natural mechanics that allow you to play dynamically. You have practiced a shot long enough so that you know it is correct and efficient, it feels really good, and the ball is going in the court. You hit the same shot over and over, sometimes from a stationary position, sometimes on the move, without much doubt as to the result. In other words, the mechanics are second nature, and you're playing dynamically, focusing on the ball and its placement.

This is the gist of my teachings. Right from the beginning, I teach you the arm movement of each stroke independent of the rest of the body. As you progress, the body starts to help the effort in a natural way.

If your stroke is poor, your attention has to be focused on the mechanics. That is why a beginner needs to think of the stroke simply as the movement of the arm independent of the legs. Otherwise, it becomes confusing and complicated. This is the main problem with conventional tennis teaching. Conventional mechanics have too many unnecessary and unnatural additions that distract you.

Therefore, don't blame yourself for **unforced errors** (lost points that your opponent did not force on you by skillful placement or sheer force). Unforced errors are usually the result of technical flaws, such as falsely enforced mechanics, rushing the timing, or an inappropriate racquet angle when making the hit.

Study this book and take the time to practice all of the drills, so you can move past mechanics to enjoy the dynamics of this beautiful game! •

How to Hit the Ball

An obvious need in hitting the ball is to clear the net, which means you have to overcome the force of gravity that is constantly pulling the ball downward. You have three options:

- Lift the ball over the net with an upward pull of the racquet as you stroke the ball, rather than just a forward motion
- Angle the racquet face slightly upward
- Use both lifting and angling techniques at the same time (but hit the ball gently or it will sail out over your opponent's baseline) (see photo next page)

Key to these modern, professional hitting techniques is bending the arm on impact with the ball. The obvious reason is that you involve large muscle groups and so achieve more power. Beginners can benefit greatly from applying this basic technique from the get-go.

THE FLIGHT OF THE BALL

The tennis ball can fly at well over 100 miles per hour in the hardest pro serves. But no matter how hard it is hit, the ball loses speed during flight because of its size and rough, unaerodynamic covering. It also slows down considerably after it bounces. A player at one baseline can hit a ball at 60 mph, and by the time it bounces and reaches the opponent's baseline, it may be traveling only 25 mph or slower.

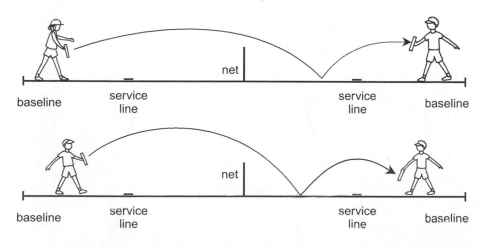

We use specific muscles as the main driving force behind strokes. As these muscles contract, they provide the power for your swing. Your biceps and triceps are located in your upper arm. The biceps flex your forearm (bend it, as in the forehand), and the triceps extend your forearm (straighten it, as in the serve). The pectorals are muscles in the chest that assist with the forehand. The trapezius run from the back of the neck and cover each shoulder, assisting with the one-handed backhand.

A fast ball drops down with less arc.

A slow ball drops down more steeply, before and after the bounce.

Your arm and the racquet angle help lift the ball over the net. The more you open the face of the racquet, the higher the ball travels.

To develop feel for the ball, have someone gently throw you some balls and hit them back with your hand instead of a racquet. Practice hitting the ball back gently with:

- Only a forward motion of your arm
- A forward arm motion plus a slight upward angling of your hand
- A forward motion of your arm, an upward pull—bending your arm—plus a slight upward angling of your hand
- A forward and upward motion of your arm, bending it and controlling the height of the ball by the angle of your hand

In each case, carefully notice where the ball goes. Keep this drill simple. You're only establishing what happens to the ball when you hit it in certain ways. As you begin playing tennis, you'll see that most ground strokes include an upward motion, not just a forward swing.

This is worth illustrating to clarify what happens when you do these motions with a racquet. •

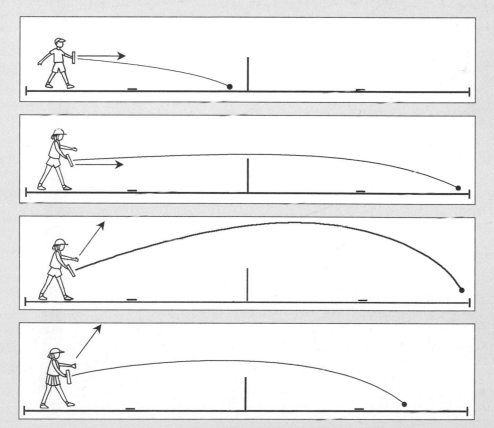

Forward arm motion only, racquet face vertical.

Forward arm motion, angled racquet (open).

Forward and upward arm motion (bending it), angled racquet (open).

Forward and upward arm motion (bending it), racquet face nearly vertical.

Observe a ball's speed after it bounces. The slower the ball is coming toward you, the more it curves downward before and after the bounce.

As you play, you will be able to coordinate your timing and movement with these arcs. The techniques in this book will teach you to wait and judge the ball *after* the bounce before committing to a swing. Incorrectly anticipating the character of the second critical arc before the ball even bounces is one of the most common causes of mis-hits. Do not try to make up your mind early. Look and follow.

TOPSPIN

You may start noticing that the ball has a slight forward rotation to it, called *topspin*. Topspin is the result of lifting the arm and racquet more than needed to clear the net. The ball rolls down the face of the racquet while being raised up by the upward motion of the racquet. To avoid hitting the ball too high with this technique as you play with more power, close the racquet face over the ball. This generates tremendous forward ball rotation—topspin. (The opposite action—the ball rolls up the face of the racquet while the racquet is going down—is called a *slice shot*. For more, see The Backhand Slice section, pages 124–28.) The more you get under the ball and lift your arm on the stroke, the more topspin you can achieve with the ball. Creating two or three rotations of the ball before it bounces in the other court is enough topspin for you at this stage. Using a little topspin when you first start playing will teach you this feel early in your tennis career and make it much easier for you to add more topspin later.

PLAY LIKE THE PROS

IMPROVE BY WATCHING

After learning the techniques in this book, watch your favorite pros use them and then mimic their strokes.

Keep your eyes on the player rather than the ball. Notice how players adjust to faster shots by keeping the swing shorter and the racquet closer to the ball.

By keeping your eyes on the player instead of following the ball, you'll catch many details, such as how long players track the ball and, finding it slowly, then accelerate and follow through. You'll notice that the arm is usually pulled in on impact, rather than extended. In essence, you'll be closer to feeling what they feel as they play if you watch the player and not the ball.

Another point, hardly noticeable except in slow-motion replay, is that players typically hit the ball to the side of the strings rather than on the center. They hit topspin toward the bottom of the strings, making the racquet more stable. The **torque** (the twisting force of ball contact that tries to turn the racquet in your hand) keeps the racquet closed, making the handling of the racquet easier and the shot safer. The opposite is true for volleys. Pros hit them toward the top of the racquet, helping the racquet stay open. However, volleys aren't hit as close to the frame as ground strokes, where the player relishes belting the ball.

Enjoy watching your favorite players but also study them closely so you can learn as much as you can. This book will answer any questions you may come up with during your journey to a better game. •

HIGH TOPSPIN IS MORE THAN A DEFENSIVE SHOT

A ball hit high with a lot of topspin slows down as it travels forward and up. Then the ball accelerates as it comes down, making it difficult to judge how the ball will bounce. Such a ball usually kicks high and toward the backcourt. This makes high topspin effective, even on hard courts, as an offensive shot to keep your opponent stuck in the backcourt.

Topspin is also a great tool for building confidence. When you are afraid of missing your shot, you don't have to hit a softer stroke to keep it in the court. With topspin, if you can clear the net and rotate the ball enough, you know the ball will drop in the court. Your fear doesn't show to your opponent because you don't need to slow down the ball to keep it in the court.

With topspin, you also can clear the net by a wider margin. On a flat, hard shot, you have to skim the net to keep the ball in play. By practicing topspin assiduously, even in an exaggerated way at first, you acquire the feel that the more you hit up, the more the ball comes down. For beginning, intermediate, and advanced players, and for pros who haven't mastered this topspin technique yet, learning it encourages them to hit much harder, even under pressure.

Yet another factor in competition is that ball rotation onto an opponent's racquet lessens their control of their shot.

When to Learn Topspin

The techniques used in this book to teach ground strokes develop topspin naturally, right from the beginning. Although this learning is done first at slow speeds, the swing developed is the same low-to-high stroke used by the pros.

I consider the following a very basic part of learning to play tennis well. Topspin requires that you apply much more upward force to the ball than the intended path of your shot.

If, on the other hand, you learn from the beginning to apply your force along the intended line of flight of your shot, this flat shot will become an instinctive habit that will be difficult to shake in the future. If for years you have been hitting the ball with a straight effort and relating this to the speed, height, and placement of your shot, trying now to lift your strokes with topspin will probably make you panic. You'll be afraid of hitting the ball too high and too far.

Although you may understand my point intellectually, deep inside you've been conditioned differently. You haven't instinctively built the feel that comes with topspin, knowing that the more you hit up on the ball and the more you roll it, the more it comes down. Players who have hit flat shots most of their lives and now want to hit topspin may need hundreds of hours of practice to master this new feel. By exaggerating the new style, they can succeed in time.

From the start, a beginner needs to develop the feel that lifting the stroke causes the ball to curve down. Their tennis instinct is virgin territory. Beginners who learn topspin from the start aren't afraid of hitting the ball out of the court. Whenever their shots fall beyond the baseline, they roll the next ball more. Topspin builds confidence because a player can hit harder and higher and still bring the ball down into the court. It provides a much larger margin for error when hitting a ball hard. Flat hits cause innumerable errors, lessening confidence.

As you progress as a topspin player, you'll learn to rotate the ball more and more efficiently, whether on your forehand, backhand, or serve. Should you decide to risk a few shots, you may choose to hit some flatter strokes, but you can always revert to the safer topspin shots when needed.

Follow these guidelines to fine-tune your topspin:

- The tendency in most sports is to go forward toward your intended target and to release the power too soon, thinking you don't have enough time. These two habits cause too many errors. Instead, wait a bit after the bounce, approach the ball slowly from below, almost touching it before accelerating, and stroke upward but emphasize going across the ball, in a windshield wiper arc (for more, see pages 91–95).
- Let your body go to the left rather than "stepping into" the ball.
- Use your biceps to bend your arm, bringing your racquet closer to your body, rather than extending your arm and following the line of the ball. If

you look carefully at the top pros, you'll see that they make contact toward the bottom of the racquet, below the sweet spot.

- If you are starting anew to add topspin to your forehand, end your stroke above your left shoulder (for right-handers). On two-handed backhands, hit up and across to your right, ending over your right shoulder.

- If you have a one-handed backhand, meet the ball by moving your fist toward the net, with the racquet laid back almost perpendicular to your arm. Approach the ball slowly. Accelerate on contact, up and somewhat across to your right. The nonhitting arm should move back and the shoulder blades come together, while lifting your body. You don't need to step forward into the ball. It is usually more helpful letting your body move up and slightly back. While this is different from the traditional instruction of stepping into the ball, going backward gives you more room and allows a more natural and efficient acceleration of the backhand stroke. You can confirm this by flicking a whip while pulling back and then trying it while stepping forward, and comparing the results.

- In training, exaggerate the finish of these strokes, leaving the arm up a bit, relating your finish to the landing of your shot. •

Ironically, bringing the racquet slowly to the ball, then accelerating gives you more power and control.

PUSHING THE BALL

Push means to exert pressure or force against something so as to move it. *Hit* means to give a blow to or strike something. In tennis, *pushing* the ball has been vilified as hitting the ball too softly, while *hitting* is used for stronger strokes. But in fact, you can push something with more force than you can hit it.

Imagine yourself in front of a large barrel of water. If you hit it with your hand, it will barely move. If you push it, you may tip it over. Top pros use this concept in tennis. They approach the ball slowly, almost touching it before discharging all their power. It's only when they meet the ball that most of their muscular contraction occurs. If you were to analyze their racquet-head velocity on high-speed film, you would see that the fastest part of the swing is well after contact, sometimes occurring as much as 2 feet after the impact.

Try to keep the idea of pushing in mind. The slower you approach

TOPSPIN OR FLAT?

There is a misconception that top players play flat on hard courts, meaning they hit the ball with a flat racquet face versus adding spin. The latest research, carried out during tournaments on hard court surfaces, shows that top players such as Andre Agassi and Roger Federer hit their ground strokes with plenty of topspin, well above 1,500 rpm. Pete Sampras's first serves have approached 3,000 rpm, while some of his second serves have been recorded to spin above 5,000 rpm.

Study the top players of all time, and you'll see a lot of ball rotation: Bill Tilden's and Jack Kramer's forehands, Pancho Gonzalez's serve, Don Budge's and Tony Trabert's backhands, Manuel Santana's forehand, Rod Laver's and Ivan Lendl's strokes on both sides. In the last two decades, this phenomenon has become more prevalent. Witness Andre Agassi, Boris Becker, Pete Sampras, Gustavo Kuerten, Lleyton Hewitt, Roger Federer, Justine Henin-Hardenne, Andy Roddick, and all the Spanish players. Venus Williams hits ground strokes with an average topspin of 2,000 rpm. Serena Williams, Justine Henin-Hardenne, Lindsay Davenport, Jennifer Capriati, and the Russian female players likewise tame their tremendous power with plenty of topspin sting.

Topspin is a forward roll, as if the ball were rolling forward on the ground. You create topspin by brushing up on the ball while stroking, lifting the racquet much higher than the intended line of flight of the ball.

the ball, the more you can accelerate. Force, if you remember from physics, is mass (weight) times acceleration, not mass times velocity. In addition, the pro's muscular contractions upon meeting the ball connect the weight of the body to the impact with the ball, generating even more power.

This is a subtle factor not easily seen when you watch the pros, but if you observe just the racquet head as it approaches the ball and then accelerates, you'll see how your favorite player pushes rather than hits the ball.

Even today's ultralight racquets are about five times heavier than tennis balls. Taking a hard swipe at a ball, as in baseball, results in too heavy a hit, with a resulting loss of control over its direction. You'll achieve maximum control with a ground stroke that seems first to almost touch the ball with the racquet, then accelerate, generating plenty of ball speed. Unlike baseball, where the swing of the bat speeds up well

The forward rotation of the ball makes the air friction on top of the ball considerably higher than that on the underside. The air above the ball is pushed forward, increasing the pressure on the ball and pushing it downward. The air below the ball is pushed backward by the felt of the ball, thereby separating the air molecules below the ball and creating a zone of lower air pressure that pulls it down toward the ground.

Topspin, in addition to the force of gravity, makes for a much more pronounced downward curve in the ball's flight path. The ball drops much sooner than if it had no spin at all (a "flat" ball). The faster the ball rotates forward, the more downward force it has, accelerating it as if thrown down.

Although still not widely taught at the beginner and intermediate levels, topspin is clearly a tremendous advantage to any player. It allows you to hit the ball with great force, well above the net, knowing that it will come down in the opponent's court. A topspin ball is also going to take quite a jump after the bounce, making it difficult for your opponent to advance to the net or to hit a winner from the backcourt. Furthermore, its rotation impairs your opponent's control of his shot. This happens very often at the professional level. You'll see many rallies between the top players in the world where the ball doesn't pass the service line by much, but it is still effective at keeping the other player back. The ball rotation also forces your opponent to resort to a safer shot than usual. ●

before contacting the ball, the tennis stroke starts accelerating much closer to the impact. As a beginner, think of it happening from the impact point onward.

At higher levels, tennis is not only a game of power but also a game of extreme precision and feel. This means the player tends to move the ball across the strings as if caressing it—in the same way you caress a cheek rather than slapping it.

HAND-EYE COORDINATION

Hand-eye coordination in tennis means tracking the ball with your eyes and connecting with it comfortably using your racquet. I call this *finding the ball*, and it's the most underrated factor in tennis and the most important skill to learn. Without it, you can't play well.

The forehand stroke in tennis is quite similar to catching a ball and then releasing it with an underhand throw over the net and into your opponent's court. To coordinate your catch with the flight of the ball after the bounce, you track the ball with your right hand until you grab the ball. If you rush, putting your hand out too soon or closing your fingers before the ball arrives, you'll miss the catch. If you don't follow the ball well with your eyes and hand, you'll also miss the catch.

The same goes for your strokes in tennis. If you want good control of your shots, you need to bring your racquet close to the ball before releasing your power. This is the most important skill that all top pros have mastered.

To develop your eye for the bounce and subsequent flight of the ten-

5. MASTER PUSHING

1. To see how the pros push ground strokes at speeds in excess of 60 mph, grab a small cushion and go to an open space. Have someone hold it lightly at the top corner between two fingers or place the cushion on a raised surface such as a table.
2. With your hand open, take a swing and hit the side of the pillow as hard as you can. Observe how far it moves.
3. Repeat, placing the pillow on the table. Now place your hand on the side of the pillow, barely touching it, and then push it forward and upward as hard as you can. Observe that it moves much farther. ●

nis ball and to prime your coordination for tennis, practice the drills on pages 63–67. Do them barehanded (without a racquet) by yourself or with someone else, either at home, on the court, or anywhere with a firm surface. Even if you feel competent at it, do each drill a few times to become even more familiar with the bounce and changing speeds of the ball.

You may have to do some light running while doing these drills. Do things as slowly and efficiently as you can, keeping your eyes and your attention focused on the ball in flight. If some balls are uncomfortably out of reach, just let them go; you can pick them up later. The emphasis here is on control and coordination, not speed.

FORGET YOUR FEET

Since you learned how to move your body at an early age, you have no need to relearn what you already know. At home, on the street, or at work, when you have to move to your left or right, you naturally turn and walk or run facing the direction you are heading. The same applies

WATCH OTHER PLAYERS

If you have the opportunity, watch people playing tennis at a local club or on television and observe the following:

- A forehand
- A one-handed backhand
- A two-handed backhand
- A forehand volley
- A backhand volley
- A service
- An overhead
- The racquet's approach to the ball on a ground stroke
- Acceleration of the racquet head after ball contact
- Lifting the ball
- Pushing the ball
- How the ball slows in flight and at the bounce
- How the arc after the bounce is much more pronounced
- How the ball slows by the time it reaches the other baseline •

Stand comfortably facing the net (left).

The natural, easy way to approach the ball is to turn while tracking the ball with your hand, as if intending to catch it (right).

Face the ball to find it with your hand (left).

Keep your hand up while you turn toward the center (middle).

Return to the center, ready for the next ball (right).

in tennis. Your body will move naturally to reach the ball. You want to focus your attention on connecting your racquet with the ball, nothing else. Your eyes and hand lead, your body follows.

When you catch a baseball or football, you don't think about every step or body movement. You just run fast with economy of effort and keep most of your attention on the ball and your hands as you catch it. You move toward the ball instinctively, without thinking of your feet.

TIMING AND COORDINATION

The slower you move with these slow ball speeds (see pages 63–67), the easier it will be for you to understand the mechanics of the swing, and the faster you'll be able to make adjustments at higher ball speeds as you become more skilled.

Work out your timing according to the speed of the ball coming toward you and how economically you can move. You will definitely notice if you are late in your swing because you will feel the ball is past you. If you are only slightly late, you will be able to keep the ball in play. If you are too early, you're more likely to lose control of the ball. Wait until well after the bounce before moving your racquet back and then forth to generate power. It is almost like touching the ball before hitting it.

Don't let anyone rush you. Some people may urge you to bring the racquet back early, but this will only interfere with your own timing. You need to work this out for yourself. You have all the "data" you need to judge your timing, and the quieter the world around you, the better you will do. ●

Approach the tennis ball the same way—as if you were going to catch it. You'll soon realize that in tennis the arms and hands can move independently of the rest of the body. Let your feet look after themselves and focus on the ball and your hands.

When pulled to the far edge of the court to reach the ball, top players turn and run straight to the ball. Notice this the next time you watch a tournament. In conventional coaching, you are taught to take side steps first, and then turn before you hit the ball. The side steps you sometimes see between shots at the professional level are a natural response of a well-trained athlete slowly drifting while watching to see where the opponent hits next. But demanding these side steps every time you move to the side of the court forces an unnatural motion on a player. This natural method of turning to run toward the ball is one of the techniques that sets my coaching system apart from conventional systems.

Conventional tennis teaching makes you think about the position of your feet practically all the time you're playing. This is hand-eye-**foot** coordination, which effectively destroys hand-eye coordination. Moving instinctively is one of the hallmarks of the Wegner Method.

THE DISCIPLINE OF WAITING

How do you define instinct? At the highest level of performance, perceptions come in and decisions go out at speeds too fast for the conscious mind to grasp. Ironically, you can develop this by waiting—by taking your time. Conversely, you can lose it by rushing.

In professional tennis, when the player is well focused, playing by instinct and feel, the ball can be traveling at a high velocity, but the player feels no need to rush. He looks for the ball with the racquet as if it is part of his body, an extension of his hand. Finding the ball, he explodes with power, guiding the ball over the net in the intended direction. The focus is on finding the ball and repeating a certain feel in each stroke. Basically, the pro player is trying to prevent being early, which by experience he knows is the main cause of most mistakes. The earlier you are, the more you lose feel.

Attention to the sound of each shot is equally important when focusing on feel and using the discipline of waiting. It takes the mind off distractions. That is why top pros play better when there is absolute silence during a point. They hear the opponent's stroke, the bounce, and then their own stroke. These sounds help the player focus and stay in the present time.

One of the most difficult things in tennis is to avoid rushing the shot. Even at the high speeds of a top-level game, I have counted more than 80 percent of pro errors resulting from rushing. Only a small percentage of errors came from hitting late.

To find out how much time you have after the bounce of the ball, count (silently) "1" at the bounce, then "2," "3," "4," and "5" at the hit. You'll see how much time you have.

After trying this counting drill, many players, including pros, are usually in disbelief of their former "rushing to prepare" strategy, realizing how much trouble it has created for them.

Work the other way around by finding out how you can expand the waiting time while stalking the ball. You don't want to be standing still, but beware of bringing your racquet back early. By taking your time, you'll become a smoother player and your errors will be less frequent. ●

- Toss the ball underhand higher than your head and catch it underhand on its way down (see photos below). Repeat until you can catch the ball comfortably every time.
- Toss the ball underhand higher than your head. Let it bounce up, then catch it underhand on its way down. Repeat, tossing the ball to different heights, until you can catch it smoothly every time.
- On a tennis court or other firm surface, stand about 15 feet away from your partner and have her toss the ball to you. The highest point of the toss should be about 6 feet. The ball should bounce well in front of you so that it starts to arc down by the time you catch it underhand (see top photo next page). Throw it back underhand. (If you don't have someone to work with, skip to the solo drills beginning on page 65.)
- Using the palm of your hand, practice pushing up the ball toward your partner, who catches it. Repeat until you connect with the ball every time (see middle photo next page).
- Now complete the swing of your arm with your hand ending up over your

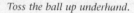

Toss the ball up underhand.

Catch the ball underhand.

Catch the ball underhand.

left shoulder, which you touch with your index finger. This accustoms you to moving your arm correctly when hitting a ball with a racquet. Your push should lift the ball above eye level and toward your partner (see bottom photo).

- Play the ball back and forth, using the palm of your right hand to push the ball over the net. (Use a table or chair placed halfway between you and your partner if you're not on a court.) Repeat until you can easily rally back and forth. Focus on finding the ball all the time and pushing it upward toward your partner, while finishing over your shoulder (see illustration).

Push the ball upward toward your partner.

Finish with the back of the hand by your cheek.

chair

Rally over a chair.

Solo Drills

- Toss the ball underhand against a wall. Let it rebound and bounce off the ground. Catch it underhand when it starts to fall toward the ground again. Catch the ball at a comfortable height, a bit below your waist. Practice increasing your distance from the wall and varying the height where you hit the wall until you can catch it smoothly every time. See photos below and next page.
- Next, rally against the wall, hitting the ball with the palm of your hand instead of catching it (see top photo next page).
- Ensure you complete the swing of your arm with your hand ending up over your left shoulder, which you touch with your index finger (see bottom photo next page). This accustoms you to bending your arm when

Hold the ball underhand and toss it.

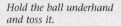

Toss the ball underhand.

Track the ball.

Catch the ball underhand.

hitting a ball with a racquet. Your push should lift the ball above eye level toward the wall.

By now, rather than rushing to hit the ball, you should be:

- Bringing your hand near the ball and a little below it
- Accelerating from the contact point onward in an upward motion
- Finishing by touching your shoulder (for more on finishing, see the sidebar on page 68)

Even if your feet are rushing to reach the ball, your arm and hand need to move smoothly to find the ball, with all your effort applied from the contact point onward.

If you have difficulty with any drill, keep working on that particular one.

Hit the ball up.

Lift and finish over the shoulder.

Reach the point where you can do it comfortably before you try to play with a racquet. •

- Have your partner throw balls to each corner of the court as you stand in the middle of the baseline. Pivot and run to catch them.
- Now try to sidestep to reach the ball. You'll quickly see how inefficient this is.
- This time have your partner send faster, deeper, and wider shots to each corner until you can reach them with zero attention on your feet and all your focus on your hand and the ball. •

FOCUSING ON THE FINISH

I have found that the key to conquering the fears and worries people have when executing any stroke in tennis is to work on always finishing the stroke in the same spot. In fact, your most important goal as you play is to finish your stroke, no matter what may happen to the ball. An incoming ball may bounce badly or unpredictably but just focus on finding it and finishing the stroke as usual. As you progress, you'll instinctively adjust the other parts of your stroke, such as the racquet angle, to guide the ball into the other court.

Focusing on the finish is one of the best-kept secrets among the top pros. It enables you to take your attention off wondering about how to connect with the ball and focus instead on sending it where you want. It also allows you to move more naturally, taking your attention off where your feet are going and putting it on the feel of the game—the feel of the racquet in your hands and the feel of the ball on your racquet strings.

Human beings tend to worry too much about the mechanics of how things are done. So don't be human. On their best days, top pros can look like gods on the court because they're focusing on feel, especially the feel of the acceleration through the ball and the finish of the stroke. Put too much attention on other areas and you'll have ten different swings. A pro's swing for each stroke (forehand, backhand, and serve) always looks the same. Each swing is always well defined, distinguished mostly by the way it ends. ●

Find the ball slightly in front of you (left).

Focusing on the finish makes it easier to put the ball where you want it (right).

PLAY WITH THE HAND

In tennis, as in many other sports, the less you think about body positions and the more you focus on the ball in the present, the more feel you'll have. Tennis pros play in the present and so should you.

Trying to judge the speed of the ball with your mind only makes tennis more difficult. But here's the secret—you don't need to judge it. Just look at the ball carefully. You'll see how much it slows down, first in the air as it comes toward you, and then appreciably more after the bounce. Research has shown that from baseline to baseline, the ball loses close to 60 percent of its speed. The ball always curves downward. The more it decreases in speed, the sharper it drops.

Take your time and become an observer as you run to the ball. Your legs may be moving fast to reach the ball, but your arm can wait far longer for the ball to come within your reach.

Tennis professionals have favorite body positions when they are not rushed to stroke. But when rushed, they readily abandon their preferences to reach the ball with the racquet; reaching the ball is their main concern, not their balance.

When a top pro has the ball within his reach, he concentrates on hitting it over the net, moving the hand independently of the rest of the body to accomplish that aim. Top pros play tennis with the hand, and the rest of the body moves instinctively to help the hand.   •

CONVENTIONAL TEACHING AND TALENT

When you watch a top tennis pro, you may marvel at her ability to place the ball regardless of the power generated by the shot. You may also admire her focus, graceful moves, demeanor, attitude, and will to win, as well as how the pro handles the power of the other player.

The skill level of these pros seems superhuman yet extremely simple and efficient. Tennis students have been led to believe they should not copy the pros, especially in the beginning stages of learning the game. But those top pros are so natural, so powerful in their tennis, why not copy their strokes?

One of the most frequent reasons people shy away from copying the top players is the consensus within the tennis teaching industry that this is an unreasonable proposition, that the techniques used by pro players are only suited to the super-gifted, to those born with an unbelievable level of skill. They recommend that you copy the top pros only **after** you are good. This is nonsense. These pros are good because they started playing the way they play.

Shying away from the extreme simplicity of a top player's game is causing severe problems in the tennis teaching profession and in the popularity of the game. And this is sad because anyone can learn tennis quickly and reach a higher level of playing by copying the best players in the world. In essence, you may be much more talented and have much more ability than you are credited with by conventional systems (or that you credit yourself with). You'll show these talents only if you start using the right techniques. •

STAY DOWN OR COME UP?

One of the most unnatural things to do while playing tennis is to force yourself to stay down through the stroke, as if you were sitting down while executing your stroke. None of the top pros do this. Why do the pros come up? Because staying down traps the swing instead of facilitating it. The body naturally wants to come up. Try swinging something resembling a pendulum from your hand and notice that if you lower your hand, the pendulum slows down. If you raise your hand, the pendulum accelerates.

Lifting from the trunk and legs helps pros accelerate the stroke. Prime examples are Andre Agassi, Serena Williams, Roger Federer, Justine Henin-Hardenne, and Lleyton Hewitt, who lift so much on the forehand stroke that often they come off the ground.

In actuality, a minimum of body lift is necessary to feel comfortable. Otherwise you'll lock up your body, twisting it forcefully, and be more prone to back and hip injuries than players who lift up. Staying down combined with the traditional closed stance on the forehand is also a major contributor to knee injuries.

If the ball is short and low or you are reaching far in front, you may need to get down to reach it. But making a player stay down for every shot is a major block to improvement. Top players develop a feel for the optimum move in a particular situation, staying down for some shots, coming up for others. This is true even for the backhand slice and volley. John McEnroe, the best net player of all time in my estimation, employed this style.

So beware of the trap of forcing yourself to stay down. Do whatever feels natural and most aids your stroke. •

the forehand

4

Maria Sharapova. [Art Seitz]

The Forehand Grip

The way you hold a racquet in your hand for a particular shot is called your *grip*. Professionals develop their own particular grips for each of their shots, making gradual adjustments during their early playing years until they find the ones that are most comfortable and effective. Players usually have a forehand grip, a backhand grip, and slight variations

Place the racquet on the ground to your right, with the head of the racquet facing forward (left).

Bring the racquet butt up against your navel, with the face vertical and the tip slightly down (right).

for serves and volleys. As you progress through this book, you will find yourself making subtle changes to your grips until you find the ones that are most comfortable for you. Then you'll automatically be able to change smoothly between one grip and another.

Placing the racquet on the ground will help you grip it comfortably when you pick it up naturally. Grasp the racquet by the handle with your right hand while keeping the racquet face vertical and touching the racquet butt against your navel. Let your fingers spread slightly apart and relax. Rest the middle of the racquet in your left hand, just above your right hand.

The position of your left hand can vary according to your liking, and may adjust itself as you continue to play. The goal is to help balance and distribute the weight of the racquet between both hands when you are not hitting the ball. While you're waiting for your opponent's next shot, hold the racquet in both hands close to the center of your body and pointing forward. This puts you in the *ready position*. Release your left hand to hit the ball. After finishing the swing, bring the racquet back into your left hand in the ready position.

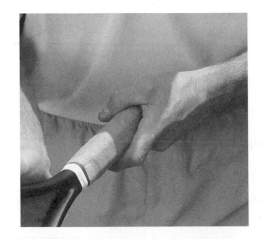

If you're left-handed, follow the same grip instructions, reversing hands, and practice the drills until you can find your grip with your eyes closed.

A few minutes with these drills will help you develop a solid, steady grip.

- Walk around the court with the racquet in the ready position until you become used to the position of your arms while you move around. Walk or jog toward both your left and right sides.
- Close your eyes while standing still. Release your right hand from the grip and reach out away from your body while keeping the racquet in position with your left hand. Bring your right hand back onto the grip, discovering the same feel as before. Practice until you can find your grip without looking at your racquet or hand.
- With your eyes still closed, release your right hand from the grip, but this time move your racquet to the left with your left hand. Bring the racquet back to the ready position and grip it again with your right hand, feeling your grip. Repeat until you have it down.
- With your eyes open, again practice releasing your right hand, reaching out to the right, and replacing your hand without looking at your grip. •

FEEL YOUR GRIP

Look ahead, not at your racquet. *Feel* the grip. There is nothing complicated about it. You don't need to think about it, and you don't need to look at it. It just needs to feel comfortable and secure, with your fingers relaxed. The racquet should point forward, with the racquet face perpendicular, or nearly so, to the ground. It should be level or have a slight downward tilt. Feel the weight of the racquet in your hand. When swinging the racquet, you vary the finger pressure, usually tightening your fingers at the moment of impact. Too loose a grip will cause you to lose control and power in your shots. Remember, you will eventually find the most comfortable and efficient grip. Don't force yourself to follow someone else's idea of what is best for you.

Note that this two-handed resting position is also the basis for the two-handed backhand grip. In this stroke, the left hand drives the shot, with the right hand fairly relaxed and maintaining the forehand grip. The only real difference is that you'll slide your left hand down toward the right hand, hitting the ball with both hands fairly close to or touching each other. (For more, see Chapter 5, The Backhand.)

THE JIM COURIER FOREHAND

Jim Courier had the strongest forehand of his time. His combination of power and topspin made him the number one player in the world in 1992. He won two Australian Opens (1992 and 1993) and two French Opens (1991 and 1992).

What made his forehand such a strong but simple shot was keeping his racquet between his body and the ball as long as possible. He followed it as if he were going to stop it in front of his face with the palm of his right hand. From there, it was easy. As soon as he felt the ball was within his grasp, he released the strongest swing possible, across his body to his left. Even his body shifted to the left, aiding this forceful punch up and across. Another trademark was his confidence in this relentless attack. He mercilessly hammered every forehand ball.

To help you understand this type of stroke, ask someone to feed you slow, high balls to your forehand side. Keep your hand and racquet pointing up and in front of you (your wrist in a cocked position). As the ball comes toward you, look at the ball through the strings as if looking at the back of your hand, not your palm. (This is an exaggerated movement. Don't think you should look at the ball through the strings in a match.)

After the bounce, just find the ball well, preferably near waist height or above, and hit it quite hard, as naturally as you can, with topspin and sidespin, shifting your body to the left (for a right-hander).

Your wrist will become used to this cocked position, giving you plenty of power and maximizing control. Do not force your wrist or tighten up too much on your grip (a cause of tennis elbow). This stroke may be helpful, but if it causes you any physical trouble, it may not be for you. ●

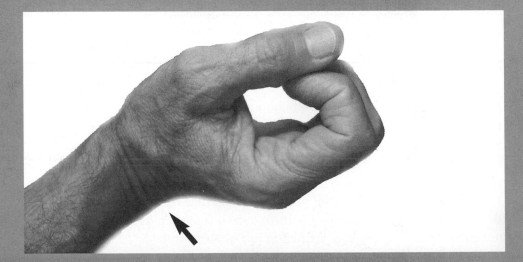

Cocked wrist position.

Forehand 1-2-3-4

The modern forehand is one of the most effective and powerful weapons in professional tennis, and the trademark of most of the best players over the past century. Students have often been discouraged from copying these incredible forehands on the grounds that they were unique to those players and almost a freak of nature, rather than a specific technique that could be learned. This is a misconception, which you'll find out as you apply the principles in this chapter.

The forehand has four easy steps.

1. Start in the ready position in the middle of the court, with your racquet near your navel.
2. Move to the ball naturally, as if you were going to catch it, holding your racquet in front of you and watching the ball.

The ready position (left).

Tracking the ball (right).

Finding the ball slowly (left).

Accelerate over your shoulder (right).

3. Find the ball slowly, positioning your racquet to connect with it slightly below the center of the strings, while already having your finish in mind.

4. Accelerate the racquet up and across your body, finishing with your hand and racquet over your opposite shoulder. Feel as if you've pushed the ball up and over the net. Remember that you create the momentum of your swing from near the point of contact with the ball onward. You also want to lead the swing with the upper edge of the racquet going up and across toward your left shoulder. Finishing is important. Make sure your racquet ends up over your left shoulder and neither stuck in front of you nor pointing at the other court. Your elbow should be fully bent and the back of your hand near your left ear.

The left-handed forehand uses the same steps, but the directions are reversed.

1. Start in the ready position in the middle of the court.

2. Move to the ball naturally, holding your racquet in front of you.

The ready position (left).

Tracking the ball (right).

Finding the ball slowly (left).

Accelerate over your shoulder (right).

3. Find the ball well, positioning your racquet to connect with it slightly below the center of the strings, while already having your finish in mind.

4. Accelerate the racquet up and across your body, finishing with your hand and racquet over your right shoulder. Feel as if you've pushed the ball up and over the net. Remember that you create the momentum of your swing from near the point of contact with the ball onward. You also want to lead the swing with the upper edge of the racquet going up and across toward your right shoulder. Finishing is important. Make sure your racquet ends up over your right shoulder and neither stuck in front of you nor pointing at the other court. Your elbow should be fully bent and the back of your hand almost touching your right ear.

Caution: Do not "break" your wrist, which can drastically affect your shot. Your wrist should be laid back slightly with the racquet's upper edge moving upward, together with your arm.

9. MASTER THE FOREHAND 1-2-3-4

Bring a friend who is good at tossing balls and a bucket with a dozen or more balls.

- To establish how balls bounce on the type of surface you're on, toss a ball back and forth over the net with your friend, letting it bounce once each time. Then play it barehanded (without a racquet) a few times.
- Now, using a racquet but no ball, practice the forehand steps until you can perform them fluidly without having to think about how to do them. Repeat with your eyes closed to increase your feel of the motion.
- Move to the middle of the court, slightly in front of the service line, facing the net (see top left photo opposite). Place your racquet in the ready position. (For an easier start, choke up and slide your right hand up on the racquet.) Have your friend stand in the opposite court near the net to toss balls to you. If you're using soft training balls, your friend can try to catch them, but if you're using regular tennis balls, he should stand to one side, leaving the middle of the court open for you to hit balls into without hitting him.
- Next, have your friend slowly toss balls a foot or two to your right side, high enough so they bounce well in front of you, are about waist high,

Get in the ready position,
slightly in front of the
service line (left).

Find the ball slowly and to
your front with the surface
of your racquet strings
(right).

and start to drop by the time
they reach you. This allows you
plenty of time to find the ball
(see top right photo). Wait for
the bounce and then for the
ball to come near you, moving
your body as little as possible.

Accelerate your right hand
and racquet up and across
your body until your hand
touches the upper part of your
left shoulder (see bottom right
photo). Make this motion with a
gentle upward pull as you
touch the ball, speeding up the
momentum of your arm from
contact with the ball onward. It
should feel like you pushed the
ball up and over the net. Lead

Finish the swing with the
racquet over your shoulder.

the swing with the upper edge of the racquet, so that it goes up and over your left shoulder. This motion should propel the ball at about 20 mph and 2 to 4 feet over the net. Do this drill forty or fifty times. Again, be gentle. Do not take a hard swing or you'll lose the feel for the stroke. As you continue to practice, you can start to slide your hand down the handle toward a normal grip position, if you like. Keep the finish over the shoulder, whether or not you are choking up on the racquet. •

Open or Closed Stance?

A key element in my teaching method differs completely from the conventional tennis teaching systems, especially with the forehand. Conventional systems demand that you turn your feet sideways to the net, facing the sideline as you hit—a *closed stance*. My system encourages you to hit facing the net—an *open stance*. See photos opposite.

Let's look at the pros. Unless they're hitting a forehand on the run, they open up their stance to face the net. Why? Because an open stance has so many benefits:

1. It's easier to hit and control the ball with your right side close to the ball.
2. You generate more power. Your body, coiled backward from the waist up, releases that energy into the ball when you naturally unwind into the open position. It's similar to twisting a spring and then letting it return to its original position. Muscles on the left side of your body help power a faster turn of your body into the ball. In a closed stance, you lack this thrust and rotational power because the body is at rest.
3. It's easier to reach the ball and maintain your balance during a

A closed stance means your feet face the sideline.

An open stance means your feet face the net.

Watch some top pros play and notice how they use an open stance for their forehands.

- Have a friend throw balls about a foot or two to your right side and practice the four forehand steps using an open stance to strike the ball. Pivot back and forth, coming back to the middle after each shot. Then practice with the balls thrown at increasing distances to your right, making you move to the balls before assuming the open stance. Come back to the middle after each shot.
- Now have your friend throw a few balls about a foot or two to your right side and practice the four forehand steps with a closed stance. Come back to the middle after each shot. Then practice with a few balls thrown at increasing distances to your right, making you move to the balls before assuming the closed stance. Come back to the middle after each shot. Isn't this uncomfortable?
- Now practice the first part of the drill again, hitting with an open stance. Once you've mastered the open stance and feel that it is easier and more effective for your forehand shots, finish with some relaxed rallying. Rally until you can play without thinking about your feet. •

powerful hit. When you hit the ball facing sideways, your hand starts the swing farther from the ball, and you have to strain to reach it, resulting in some loss of balance.

4. You can see the ball better. When you want to examine a painting, for example, it's natural for you to look at it head-on, not turned sideways.

5. After hitting the ball, you can turn back to the center more quickly and naturally, leading to better recovery, court coverage, and preparation for your next shot. When your opponent is hitting balls to one side of your court and then to the other, it takes you far too long to turn back from a closed stance. Even while running along the baseline to a ball hit far from their position, top players tend to open their forehand stance to strike, facing the net. It is a natural and highly effective response. A closed stance has to be drilled forcefully into a player.

GENERATING AND HANDLING POWER

As martial arts teaches, it's more efficient to deflect an incoming force than to oppose it. In tennis, this means that it's easier to return an incoming ball by deflecting it—distorting its path—than hitting it straight on. To achieve this, your swing moves from a relaxed state to a forceful contraction. To continue the martial arts comparison, the relaxed state is the yin and the more forceful one is the yang. The longer the yin, the more yang you can generate.

A relaxed state does not mean that your racquet is stationary. The process starts when you swing toward the ball with mild force, then suddenly switch your stroke in another direction. In this new direction, your muscles are fairly relaxed at first, but all at once you contract them powerfully (muscles are stronger when you shorten them), achieving a major force (yang) in the new direction.

Andre Agassi and Roger Federer are prime examples of these principles, especially on the return of serve. They accomplish this by hitting up and across the body, rather than following the ball forward in the follow-through. Agassi, in the later years of his career, has gone much deeper into executing these subtleties.

Another example is Andy Roddick's serve. He relaxes and contracts his triceps—a long, strong muscle—to bend and extend his arm, using the front edge of the racquet frame to address the ball, almost touching it. All of a sudden, he turns the racquet and hammers it up and to the right. The result is astonishing power without the need for too much force. His serve is an exquisitely timed contraction and release of different muscles to amplify the overall result.

Pete Sampras's serve was phenomenal. Even though not the fastest in men's tennis, his ball has been called the "heaviest" to return. He transformed some of his force into a more damaging weapon than ball speed—ball rotation. Some of Sampras's first serves rotated faster than 3,000 rpm, and some of his second serves rotated at more than 5,000 rpm. This ball rotation increases the air resistance on top of the ball and creates a vacuum below, producing a downward force that adds to the "heaviness" of the ball.

Conventional coaches usually advise you to imagine that you're stroking through five balls in a straight line with the forehand, but this makes players lose muscle power and control, and remember—control is the major goal of a great tennis player.

Be aware that the force you're applying to the ball is not straight on, but works to deflect it. On the forehand, it's better to reach the ball slowly, then almost at contact, contract your arm and swing across your body, practically missing the second or third imaginary ball in that straight line. The ball's trajectory will not be straight in and straight out of your racquet, but will follow a tiny, semicircular curve to return it from where it came, and so you achieve your martial arts effect. As a result of the muscle and weight you are applying in such a subtle way, the ball will go out faster than it came in.

Here's an example. Let's say Venus Williams serves to Serena Williams at 120 mph. By the time the ball bounces once and approaches Serena, the serve has lost about 55 percent of its speed, reaching Serena's racquet at about 54 mph (actual measurements taken on a hard court). Serena immediately deflects it with a quick flick across her body, without much strain. (Such returns have been measured at up to 80 mph.) She uses this flicking movement to deflect the ball, perhaps across the court or down the line.

What is amazing about Pete Sampras's long career—hitting cannonball serves day in and day out—is that his serving arm and shoulder have been practically injury free. He mainly used the larger, longer, stronger triceps, instead of the shorter shoulder muscles, in the most efficient and powerful way.

Agassi's long career has been similarly injury free. Although he serves differently from Sampras, the same martial arts principles apply to his delivery. And on ground strokes, Agassi and Roger Federer may be the masters of all time.

Notice how the best one-handed backhands are hit. Gustavo Kuerten, Roger Federer, Paradorn Srichaphan, Justine Henin-Hardenne, and Amelie Mauresmo contract their back muscles (bringing the shoulder blades closer together) and hit across the ball. The best sliced backhands also are hit across, using the back muscles. And on forehands and two-handed backhands, Agassi, Serena Williams, and Marat Safin achieve their tremendous power and ease by contracting their biceps and pectorals, stroking across their bodies. They bring the racquet close to the ball slowly, magnifying control, then power across, confident the ball will stay in the court.   •

ENVISION THE CONTACT POINT
BEFORE STARTING THE SWING

On the forehand, practice keeping the racquet in front of you as long as possible to help deepen your awareness of where the ball will be before you commit your swing. This will also increase the velocity of your stroke. Conversely, if you take the racquet back before knowing precisely where you are going to meet the ball, then you have to figure out during the forward motion where the exact contact will be, which disturbs your swing. This is the conventional idea of preparing early.

Instead, practice this stalking action with your racquet in front of you until you are comfortable with it. In the beginning you may think you don't have enough time to do this. But as you do it over and over, you'll be amazed at the results. Try combining this with counting silently to 5: "1" at the bounce, then "2," "3," "4," a little pause, and hit at "5."

Track the ball with your racquet in front and then take your swing, finishing up and across your body. You may have a windshield wiper topspin (see pages 91–95), finishing around your hip, or a higher finish, ending above the shoulder. Either is fine.

Don't take the racquet back early, then track the ball, and then take a swing. This creates a flawed swing that is too tight and mechanical. It would be like answering someone before they finished asking a question. And it's awkward, especially when done too often.

Apply the same technique—stalking the ball with your racquet in front of you—to the two-handed backhand. On the one-handed backhand, track the ball with the butt of the racquet, without taking your arm back all the way. Wait for the bounce, then time your swing and finish all the way.   •

Natural
Footwork

Synchronizing your whole body to your strokes is an instinctive process you will refine by practicing the drills in this book. The more naturally you move, as naturally as if walking down the street or window-shopping, the better you will play. The tennis court is quite small. You can cover it all by taking only three or four steps to each side and a few more to move forward or backward.

In a game, you will need to hurry sometimes, just as you would speed up at a pedestrian crossing when the light starts to blink and the waiting vehicles rev their engines. Many players start their swing before they run, thereby losing valuable time that would be better used reaching to the ball. Swing preparation should occur on the run, after the bounce of the ball.

With practice, your arms will begin to feel independent of the position and movement of the rest of your body. Your body will instinctively adjust its balance to help the motion of your arm. You will be able to find the ball easily, move through the swing, and finish smoothly whether you are on the run, falling forward or backward, or completely stationary and facing the net.

Remember to keep your racquet comfortably in front of your body while running to where you will hit the ball. Focus on tracking the ball with your eyes and your racquet hand as you're moving. (*Tracking* is the coordination of your racquet with the flight of the ball so as to meet it in the right place.) Observe how the ball arcs after the bounce and how it loses speed, so you can find it perfectly. Finish your stroke with your hand and racquet over your opposite shoulder. Finally, leave the racquet in the finish position while you turn back toward the center position to reinforce the finish and relate this finish to where you placed the ball.

Do not bring your racquet back early as many conventional teachers recommend. Wait until well after the ball has bounced before starting your swing.

- Start from the service line. Have your friend toss balls slightly short so that you have to move forward to stroke them. You will be walking forward continuously while he tosses shorter and shorter balls. Find the ball slowly with the racquet as you're moving forward and finish by touching your opposite shoulder at the finish. This is your forehand swing, whether you're moving or stationary. You can add momentum by slightly increasing the swing length.

- Have your friend toss balls as you walk backward. The tosses should be long enough to force you to move back to hit them comfortably.

- Start from the left sideline, close to the service line (young children should start a bit closer to the net, according to their build, age, and coordination). Turn to your right, and start walking parallel to the net. Have your friend toss a ball a little in front of you so that you can hit it while walking (just as if walking down the street). Emphasize your finish of the stroke. Your friend also walks across his side of the court, a little behind you so you have an open court to hit into. You should hit four or five balls. (Hitting open stance is not emphasized here because you are practicing hitting on the run.)

- Now walk backward from the right sideline to the left sideline while hitting only forehands. Your friend tosses the ball close to you so that you have to move back before hitting each ball, which teaches you to put some distance between you and the ball when it is coming too close to you or right at you.

- Now hit four or five balls while walking forward, then four or five balls while walking backward. You'll have to walk slower or faster to find the ball, depending on the speed and placement of your friend's toss and where you want to meet the ball. Remember, the action is still like catching a ball, whether you have to run to reach it or not. Always find it first and don't rush the stroke.

- To work on **pivoting**—turning quickly while leaning to go in one direction, then turning and leaning to go in the opposite direction—place a can of balls in the center of the court between the service line and the baseline and stand in front of it. Your friend tosses a ball to your right, a few feet from you. Move toward it, always walking or running forward, not sideways or backward. Reach and hit the ball. Emphasize the finish of your stroke by leaving the racquet on your shoulder for a couple of steps as you head back to the center of the court, passing behind the can and looping back to your right. Always go around the can from behind so you can see your opponent's court at all times. (Don't turn your back toward your friend or the net at any time.) End up back at your original spot in front of the can, turning to your right for the next ball. See photos this page and opposite.

• Next, move the can a little closer to the baseline. Have your friend toss the ball

Stand in front of the can.

Move toward the ball.

Reach and hit in an open stance.

Keep your racquet up at the finish of your stroke as you pivot and take the first few steps back.

Move around the can in a clockwise direction.

Turn again to move to your right.

deeper and farther from you, slowly increasing the difficulty until you have the movement down and the stroke smooth, finishing the stroke over your shoulder every time.

Your friend should toss the next ball only when you're back in the middle and starting to move back to your right. He should throw it at a speed and in a direction that is not too challenging for you to reach. A ball tossed too far away or too fast or before you are ready could end up ruining your swing. Always remain in control of what you're doing. You may have to do some running to reach the ball, but return slowly to the middle. If you start losing control, return to an easier drill. Concentrate on finding the ball well and finishing the stroke properly. If you can't, your friend should either use a slower toss or throw a ball closer to your reach, or both.

- To add one more level of difficulty, have your friend feed you the balls using a tennis racquet (but only if he can control the ball with the racquet). Emphasize the following:

    Run in a relaxed way to intercept the ball

    Keep your racquet in front of you as the ball bounces

    Slow down, open your stance, and wait for the ball, still stalking it with your racquet in front

    With little backswing, find the ball gently, adding momentum to your swing

    Accelerate the arm on contact, bending it a bit forcefully when you touch the ball

    Finish your stroke with your right thumb touching your left shoulder

    Leave your hand there while you turn toward the middle of the court, observing where you placed the ball in your opponent's court

    Bring your racquet down gently toward your left hand while slowly returning to the center of the court

    Circle behind the can and resume your original position in front of it, ready for the next shot

    Practice until your motions are smooth and easy •

Windshield
Wiper Topspin

With today's formidable racquets offering so much power, top tennis pros use a *windshield wiper motion* (bending the arm across to the left so the racquet face sweeps flat across in an arc in front of your face) on their forehands to produce topspin and force the ball down within the lines. The incoming force is deflected and used to accelerate the ball in the opposite direction.

The windshield wiper motion slides the ball across the strings so it's in contact with more string surface before leaving the racquet, providing a longer feel. By bringing your arm across the body, you are contracting large muscle groups in the arms and chest, thus connecting more body weight to the racquet and generating more power with less effort. Learning this technique is easier at slower speeds. The slower you bring the racquet to the ball and then accelerate, the more pronounced the feel of these actions will be for you.

Conventional tennis teaches players to hit the ball head-on and have it bounce straight off the racquet. The problem with this approach is the arm becomes tired because the impact is straight on, putting more stress on the muscles and joints, and the player develops a much shorter feel for the ball.

The windshield wiper motion also creates *sidespin*. Upward and sideways forces cause the ball to spin on a diagonal axis and arc downward and sideways. The downward curve is obviously the most pronounced, being the effect of both the spin and gravity.

This technique is an advanced part of your development and may occur naturally. To achieve this deflecting effect you need to get under the ball with the racquet and bring the racquet up and across your body. As you become more proficient with this motion, the racquet may not always end up positioned over the left shoulder. It may finish lower on your left side. Do whatever feels natural, as long as your hand ends up on your left side, not straight ahead of you. See photos pages 92 and 93.

Young players, as well as adults new to the game, need to build strength in the wrist and forearm of their hitting arm before attempting to use the windshield wiper motion with the ferocity of big hitters.

Get under the ball with the racquet (left).

Hit the ball, bringing the racquet up and across your body and up toward your left side (right).

Some professional players, especially those who hit the backhand one-handed, have a noticeable difference between the size of their hitting arm and the other. Rod Laver and Guillermo Vilas, two former top players, had hitting arms that looked almost double the size of their other arm.

Big hitters with topspin strokes use the wrist and forearm, as well as the biceps and pectorals, to move the racquet from below the ball all the way across to the left and down on the other side. The wrist doesn't flip forward, but the forearm rotates to the left, so the fingers move similarly to when you're waving at someone. When Gustavo Kuerten was a

young boy, I coached him to finish his forehand over the shoulder. Gradually, in his later teens, he started to develop so much windshield wiper movement that the racquet did not go over his shoulder, but down the other side. His elbow also finished higher or level with the right hand. Kuerten's success is testament to the power of this technique.

Finish in a natural way, even if the racquet finishes low.

12. MASTER WINDSHIELD WIPER TOPSPIN

- Stand in front of a wall, fence, or other flat, vertical surface with your hand down to your right and the palm facing forward. Then sweep your hand up and across the surface, ending on your left side—like a windshield wiper. See photos next page.
- Repeat, using a racquet. The racquet should skim across the surface of the wall. See photos page 95.
- Once you're comfortable with the motion, stand near the baseline, facing the net, and have a friend feed you balls. Hit them with a slight windshield wiper motion, finishing over your shoulder. Then try finishing a bit lower, near your shoulder or upper ribs. Alternate between the two finishes until you can choose the one that feels better to you and produces the best results. •

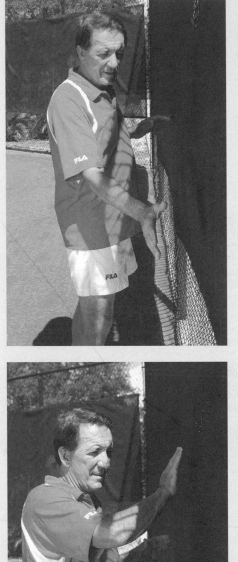

Start with your palm facing the fence, fingers pointing down (left).

Lift your hand across the surface of the fence in a windshield wiper motion (right).

Continue to sweep your hand across the front of your body (left).

Continue rotating your forearm as you finish the stroke on the other side (right).

Start with the racquet below your hand, facing the fence (left).

Lift the racquet across the surface of the fence in a windshield wiper motion (right).

Continue to sweep the racquet in an arc across the front of your body (left).

Continue rotating your forearm as you finish the stroke on the other side (right).

LESS IS MORE

What's the difference between a hacker who's still unskilled and a pro? You may have wondered about this before, and you may have also heard that no amateur can play like a pro. Not true!

The most fundamental difference is that pros seem to have one forehand style, one backhand, one serve, and so on, while most amateurs seem to have several of each, depending on the urgency of the situation, and apparently not always within their control.

If you watch players at your local club, after a few minutes you can tell if they're skilled or not. They may not be pros, but the skilled ones don't have a different forehand for each situation. Most players build this simplicity and consistency through years of experience, but with my method you can do it in days rather than years.

How is this possible? The answer is simple. The way top pros hit is the most efficient, and they use it for almost every situation, even emergencies.

I have analyzed the best shots in the game since the 1930s (the early ones on film). I've seen the progress through the decades, each generation of champions better and more complete than the one before. I have isolated what to learn from each.

If you learn each stroke in the way we've discussed—timing each stroke by waiting until the last minute instead of preparing early—what you learn will show up in any situation on the court, even the most dramatic. If you prepare too early, you'll have too much time to think and you may overreact with some outrageous stroke movement. By waiting, your basics, being the only ones you've practiced until they're second nature, will guide you to make the same moves time after time.

In normal life when under pressure or when something unexpected takes them by surprise, people usually overreact. The same can happen in competitive tennis unless you keep your cool, restrain yourself from overreacting, and repeat the particular moves that work for you, over and over.

Sometimes players overreact because they don't know the best solution to meet the situation, or they haven't practiced the right move well enough while discarding the others. This is what my method achieves: it teaches you to play like a pro. Even someone who has played for years can relearn certain skills and then look like a pro—cool, collected, and marvelously efficient. Each person's innate potential and ability can be brought out by these techniques. Simple ideas, but powerful in anyone's hands. ●

THE TRUTH ABOUT THE "WRAP"

"Show me the butt of the racquet!" is what a good coach should say when teaching a forehand finish. Visit almost any junior tennis academy, and you'll see dozens of eager younger players whipping the racquet head up and over the shoulder, pointing the butt of the racquet at the instructor at the end of the stroke. Previously, many coaches discouraged this.

However, this wrap follow-through is rapidly gaining acceptance among players and coaches as the key to racquet-head acceleration in the topspin forehand and two-handed backhand. In this technique, the racquet goes across the line of the shot, rather than forward toward the net, reaching a characteristic finish position with the arm **wrapping** across the body. The racquet has already moved to the left on the forehand and to the right on the two-handed backhand, instead of extending along the line of the ball.

All the top players have big wrap finishes, so there's no reason other players shouldn't copy them. The wrap isn't the effect of a good forehand, it's the cause. By beginning to wrap the finish, junior players are changing the fundamental shape of their swings in a way that has significantly positive consequences. Their forehands are similar to those of top pros. Video analysis shows there are no critical differences. Players such as Gustavo Kuerten, Marat Safin, Serena Williams, Justine Henin-Hardenne, Andy Roddick, Roger Federer, and Lleyton Hewitt all have a remarkable wrap, hitting across the ball through the contact zone.

The contraction of the biceps and pectorals is the driving force in the forehand and the two-handed backhand. Moving the racquet along the line of the shot, the traditional recommendation, weakens this muscle contraction, which is the critical factor in racquet-head acceleration and ball speed. Most of the muscle-contraction effort in the wrap is expended diagonally upward and across the body (not forward) to counteract the downward force of gravity and the power of the incoming ball. These two motions (upward and across) combine to give the ball topspin and sidespin as well as forward velocity.

This spin can be seen in very young players, whose steeper swing planes often generate a lot of topspin, although their balls don't penetrate the court much. But give them time. They're just learning to tame the physical universe and beginning to feel powerful. They're not holding back on force for fear of errors, and they're developing strength. As they grow bigger and stronger, the force can appear without a loss of control. •

FOCUS ON THE FINISH

Tennis is a game of movement, and perhaps no other motion is as critical as the finish. As you stroke the ball by instinct and feel, use your mind to reinforce one thing: finishing your swing. Picture the position of your arm at the end of the swing and repeat that position over and over. Leave the racquet in this finish position for a moment while you watch where your shot lands. Continue to leave it there even while turning and recovering. Relate the position of your racquet to the placement of the ball to clearly see the cause and effect: the racquet is up here, the ball landed there. Easy! Confidence builds.

The best way to minimize distractions and focus your mind is to track the ball into your racquet as long as possible, trying to see the seams of the ball. Then finish the stroke fully and leave your racquet in the finish for a moment. This will calm your fears and keep you from freezing up or changing the motion halfway through the stroke. You may swing slow or fast, but make sure your racquet goes all the way to the finishing position. Repeat this each time.

Observe Andre Agassi, Roger Federer, Gustavo Kuerten, Justine Henin-Hardenne, Venus and Serena Williams, Lleyton Hewitt, Jennifer Capriati, and Lindsey Davenport. These pros finish every shot.

On the volley, which is more of a punch, this picture of the finish is the impact point, when the ball and the racquet meet. A prime example of this is John McEnroe, the showman of the 1980s, and perhaps the best volleyer of all time.

If you are just learning this finish technique, practice your ground strokes by simply finding the ball, tracking it onto your racquet, feeling it on your strings, and pushing it over the net while finishing your stroke. No power yet; mainly feel. Repeat this until it becomes second nature. Let the power of your strokes increase gradually. You'll feel how to hit the ball harder and harder without losing control.

Paying attention to something else (such as foot position) will negatively affect your hand-eye coordination. This "distraction" takes something you learned by feel, instinctively, at a very young age, and makes you think about it, flooding your mind with unnecessary information. Tests have shown that players begin to resemble marionettes when they try to work out which foot to put where, and when. And while they're worrying about that, the ball may hit them on the head!

Another all-too-common habit that can interfere with the finish is taking your racquet back too soon. This also clouds the thought process because it forces you to imagine and adjust to the ball's path ahead of time. Bringing your racquet back early separates it from the path of the ball, killing your timing, coordination, and ease of play.   ●

Forehand Rally

A long rally implies control, yet most players taught conventionally have trouble sustaining a rally of more than a few shots. One of the many benefits of my method is being able to keep the ball in play. Students of the Wegner Method have not had their hand-eye coordination disrupted because they haven't been taught to focus on where and how to place their feet. When you pay attention to your hand and the ball and let the rest of the body move naturally, your hand-eye coordination blossoms, and your tennis skills will progress exponentially.

I have coached thousands of people, and more than 90 percent already had a good deal of coordination. Some needed a little "refresher course," spending more time on the earlier drills. However, better than nine in ten of my beginner students learned to keep the ball in play, looking smooth and with a nice finish of the stroke within an hour or two.

If you have successfully mastered the earlier drills, you are ready for the forehand rally. You need a partner who has comparable or better skills than you. Your partner must agree to rally the ball at a deliberate, slow-to-medium pace, and only to your forehand side, close enough for you to reach without straining. With no one slamming the ball or hitting it to your backhand side, rallies of fifty or more shots shouldn't be unusual.

At this stage you want to learn to put the ball where your partner can reach and return it. You are learning to aim, and this is best learned by rallying—keeping the ball in play. Most beginners try to hit the ball so hard that their opponent can't return it, thus there's

Your game is in your hands.

• Stand midway between the service line and the baseline (or closer to the service line if you prefer). Hit balls back and forth using only your forehand, making sure you hit only to your partner's forehand if you're both at the same level. Hit at a slow pace, finding the ball well, lifting it a few feet over the net with a nice finish. Always pivot to return at least a couple of steps toward the center after each hit, taking your time. Remember to leave your racquet up at your finish position for a step or two, while you are watching where the ball went, then pivot again to go for the next shot. When you can hit ten or twenty balls back and forth without errors, move farther back on the court. Gradually increase the speed to a medium-paced rally. •

no rally. This isn't the best way to learn, and it's certainly not fun to play for five seconds and then spend the next twenty seconds (or five minutes, if it went over the fence) picking up another ball to hit.

You'll find there is plenty of time between each of your hits because the ball slows down considerably in flight and during the bounce. In a slow-paced rally, the ball can take about four seconds from the time you strike it to the moment it comes back onto your racquet again. This is plenty of time to finish your stroke all the way, take a few steps back toward the middle, turn again, and find the ball when it comes back to your court. So emphasize waiting, moving slowly, and maintaining control.

Don't tighten your hand too much on the grip. Relax it between hits. You should be feeling the racquet, not gripping it tightly. Swing smoothly and firmly, without losing the feel of lifting the ball and completing your swing.

As you improve, all the small adjustments you make to intercept the incoming ball and send it on its way again—such as body motion and position—will start happening instinctively. They'll build automatically if you keep your focus on finding the ball and finishing your stroke.

Bjorn Borg, one of the top players of all time, aptly said that the essence of tennis is "to hit the ball over the net one more time than your opponent." But the next time you hit some balls around, try to keep your rally going.

INSTINCT AND FEEL

To handle something well you need to pay attention to it. You can place your attention on many things at once or focus on just one thing at a time. An interesting phenomenon in tennis is that when you focus on one thing almost exclusively—the most important factor for that situation—everything else automatically aligns with that thing. You won't need to think of two things at once. This occurs especially when you operate by feel. Playing tennis only on a conscious level, thinking of several mental images of consecutive body positions, is too mechanical and slow.

Pros operate on an instinctive level, avoiding stray thoughts as much as possible. They focus on the ball and on the finish. They remember a stroke by the way it feels, not how it looks. They don't look into their mind to recall its mechanics. They play by feel, consciously slowing down their mind, or calming it by placing all their attention on observing and feeling the ball. Breathing and walking are things you do instinctively; they are smooth and effortless (usually!), unlike taking an exam, for example, which can require great mental effort.

Judge each of your strokes by these simple criteria: Does it feel natural? Does it keep the ball in the court? Do I vaguely resemble my favorite pro (who has obviously mastered the stroke)? By copying your favorite pro you can benefit from all the years of practice he or she needed to perfect feel and technique. If that pro's stroke doesn't work well for you, emulate the stroke of another pro. By imitating their strokes, you can learn in a few days what it took them years to achieve.

The simpler you make your task, the easier it is to know what to practice and put your attention on and what not to focus on. Again, you need to trust your instincts and develop feel. As you play more and more, you'll feel how ineffective it is to strike the ball head-on—it doesn't stay on your strings much, and the feel is too short. Brushing the ball up with topspin makes it stay on your strings much longer. Striking the ball away from the center of the racquet increases your feel for the ball. Focus on repeating what feels best. •

the backhand

Gustavo Kuerten. [Art Seitz]

The Backhand Grip

YOU CAN EITHER grip the racquet with one hand or two hands to hit a backhand but you don't need to make an immediate decision on this. It's a matter of personal preference. Unless you already have an idea of which type of backhand you prefer, try some tests using your left hand. Bounce the ball left-handed, play it back and forth barehanded against a wall, or hit a few balls over the net with your left hand. If this feels comfortable, consider adopting a two-handed backhand. If it doesn't feel comfortable, you're probably better off trying a one-handed backhand first (see pages 114–22). You may come back to the two-hander later if you're curious.

The Two-Handed Backhand

The two-handed backhand is easier for children to learn because it gives them more strength and doesn't require a grip change. Many of the current top pros, who learned the two-handed backhand at an early age, perfected it into an awesome shot fit for a professional career. Other pros, starting with a two-hander, decided to switch to the one-handed stroke early in their junior years.

A two-handed backhand provides power similar to a one-handed backhand but with a shorter stroke, making it easier to make minute adjustments. Because it works the left side of the body, it also develops a more balanced body. The only disadvantage is a slight reduction in reach compared to the one-handed backhand, but this is offset by several advantages. If you hit the two-handed backhand in an open stance, it's easier to recover toward the center. It also can be hit powerfully with almost no backswing. And your arms can be bent, which makes returning a ball close to your body or a high bouncing ball easier. Both of these are more difficult to return with a one-handed backhand.

Most top players who use a two-handed backhand also employ a one-handed backhand slice (chop under the ball with the racquet) to reach a ball that is too far away for a two-handed stroke.

THE TWO-HANDED BACKHAND GRIP

Hitting a two-handed backhand is like hitting a forehand with your left hand while keeping the right hand on the racquet. The left hand does most of the work while the right hand steadies the racquet.

To establish your grip, place the butt of the racquet against your navel. The right hand stays in the same position as the forehand stroke, toward the bottom of the grip. The left hand holds the grip above the

These are similar to the hand-eye coordination drills on pages 63–67 applied to the left hand since most right-handers need to improve their left-hand dexterity. (If you're left-handed, practice these with your right hand.)

- Toss the ball underhand higher than your head and catch it underhand on its way down. Repeat until you can catch the ball comfortably every time.
- Toss the ball underhand higher than your head. Let it bounce up, then catch it underhand on its way down. Repeat, tossing the ball to different heights until you can catch it smoothly every time.
- Throw the ball against a wall and catch it with your left hand (palm up) after it bounces, preferably on its way down. You can also have someone toss you balls.
- Practice hitting the ball back and forth against a wall with the palm of your left hand.
- Repeat this last drill, but finish with your left elbow up and your left hand over your shoulder, with the back of your hand facing your right ear, which mimics the topspin racquet motion. ●

right hand, fairly close or even touching it (see top photo opposite). Some players change the right-hand position a bit, but it is not necessary for the effectiveness of the shot unless you feel more comfortable doing so. At this point, relax your hands and feel the weight of the racquet as you let the head of the racquet drop slightly. Have your fingers extended somewhat to give you more comfort and feel of the ball as it contacts the strings.

THE TWO-HANDED BACKHAND 1-2-3-4

The two-handed backhand has four easy steps:

1. Start in the middle of the court, waiting for the ball in the ready position, with your racquet butt touching your navel.
2. Turn and move to the ball naturally when you notice it coming to your left side. As you first pivot and start moving, slide your left hand down the grip until it touches your right hand. The racquet face is fairly vertical at this point. Your two-handed backhand grip is now complete.

In the two-handed backhand both hands are close to each other.

The ready position (left).

Pivot and move naturally (right).

3. Give yourself some room after the bounce. As you are about to hit the ball, open your stance, facing toward the net and the ball. Find the ball well with your racquet so that you connect with the ball slightly below the center of the string bed. You already have the above-the-shoulder finish in mind.
4. Bend your arms, accelerating the racquet all the way over the

Hit open stance (left).

Finish over your shoulder (right).

shoulder and emphasizing the over-the-shoulder finish. This finish should find your left elbow slightly higher than the right elbow, with the back of the left hand toward your right ear.

The left-handed backhand uses the same steps, but the directions are reversed:

1. Start in the middle of the court, waiting for the ball in the ready position, with your racquet butt touching your navel.
2. Move to the ball naturally when you notice it coming to your right side. As you first pivot and start moving, slide your right hand down the grip until it touches your left hand. The racquet face is fairly vertical at this point. Your two-handed backhand grip is now complete.

The ready position.

Pivot and move naturally (left).

Hit open stance (right).

3. Give yourself some room after the bounce. As you are about to hit the ball, open your stance, facing toward the net and the ball. Find the ball well with your racquet so that you connect with the ball slightly below the center of the string bed. You already have the over-the-shoulder finish in mind.

4. Bend your arms, accelerating the racquet all the way over the right shoulder and emphasizing the over-the-shoulder finish. This finish should find your right elbow slightly higher than the left elbow, with the back of your right hand toward your left ear.

Finish over your shoulder.

the backhand • 107

OPEN-STANCE BACKHANDS

The easiest way to hit a two-handed backhand is facing the net—an open stance. Your hands are closer to the ball, enabling you to reach it better and giving you more control of the shot. Although many pros hit the two-handed backhand starting in a position sideways to the net (a closed stance), those who use an open stance can drive more efficient shots and wait until the last second to change the direction of their shot. For beginners, a closed stance makes it quite awkward to reach the ball, and it may feel like an imposition, rather than the natural thing to do.

CONTROLLING THE TWO-HANDED BACKHAND

As with the forehand, the easiest and fastest way to move for a distant ball on your backhand side is to pivot and face the direction you're running in and then face the net (if possible) as you hit the shot.

If you are at a dead run across court and turning

Open stance: feet facing the net.

Closed stance: feet sideways to the net.

- Using your racquet, repeat the steps of the two-handed backhand without a ball until your motion is fluid and feels natural every time. Lead the stroke with the upper edge of your racquet as you bring it up. Accelerate upward and across your body. Let the path be dictated by what feels most natural, but keep in mind the emphasis on your finish.

- Have a friend stand near the net while you stand about 12 feet away. Have him toss balls a foot or two to your left side, fairly slowly, and about 6 feet at their highest points, so they bounce 4 or 5 feet in front of you and come up comfortably to waist height. Start in the ready position. Reach each ball and lift your shots at least a couple of feet over the net, finishing over your shoulder as usual. Since the balls are close to your reach, you don't have to run and can maintain your open stance. Repeat thirty or forty times. Become familiar with keeping your hands near your waist while waiting for the ball, and then adjust as needed. Find the ball primarily with your left hand. Follow through over the right shoulder, leaving the racquet there for a second, while looking to see where your shot has landed. ●

toward the net is just about impossible, do your best to finish your stroke while keeping your stride. Pivoting to your right is the fastest way to change direction and get back to the center of the court.

THE TWO-HANDED BACKHAND RALLY

Now you are ready to rally with your friend, backhand to backhand, hitting the ball to your partner's backhand as much as possible. This can be accomplished by angling your racquet to the right slightly.

Return a bit toward the center after each stroke, keeping your racquet over your shoulder as long as possible to reinforce the finish. Focus on finding the ball and finishing the stroke. Keep to a slow pace to start until you can rally the ball at least twenty to thirty times without a miss. Then increase your shots to a medium pace.

GETTING ON TOP OF TOPSPIN

When you learn strokes with the Wegner Method, topspin develops naturally both in your forehand and two-handed backhand. Once you can

• Put a can of balls in the center of the court behind the service line and stand in front of it. Now turn left and start walking while your friend tosses the ball in front of you. Track the ball with your racquet butt in front of your navel. Open your stance toward the net prior to finding the ball with the racquet. Determine the height and direction of your shot with the angle of the racquet. At slow speeds, you may need to open the racquet angle slightly. Lift and push the ball over the net, swinging slowly at first, always in control. Do not slap at the ball, changing the angle of your wrists. Instead, move your hands smoothly through the stroke, feeling the lift you are giving to the ball. Follow through over your right shoulder. Pivot right immediately and return toward the can, keeping the racquet in your finish position. This firmly establishes in your mind the relationship between the finish of your stroke and the ball placement in your opponent's court. Look at the ball over your shoulder to see where it landed. Never turn your back to your opponent after the hit.

Turn to your right after your shot and walk back toward the can. Cut around behind the can to circle it counterclockwise (making a figure-eight pattern). After you move around the can from the backcourt, turn to your left and move in front of the can for the next ball. When you again begin walking toward the left side of the court, your friend tosses you another ball. Af-

Track the ball with your racquet (left).

With an open stance, adjust the angle of your racquet and lift the ball over the net (right).

Keep your racquet over the shoulder while returning to the middle and watching where the ball went (left).

Bring the racquet back to your navel as you are rounding the can (right).

ter a while, the stroke will become quite automatic, going from the ball to the shoulder, whether the ball is high or low, close to you, or away from you. See photos opposite and this page.

- When you're hitting comfortably from near the service line, move the can farther back toward the baseline a few feet at a time. Then have your friend toss the ball slightly farther to your left each time to make you reach for it. Hit and pivot back to the center while holding the finish and watching where you placed your shot. Always increase the difficulty of any drill very slowly, so you can still feel the ball and the finish of the stroke. •

Loop around the can to go for the next ball.

hit topspin on both sides consistently from the backcourt at a medium pace and 3 to 6 feet over the net, you are on the way to becoming a good player. Topspin is widely used by the best players. I encourage you to use topspin right from the beginning so you have the best stroke production to play consistently and look like a pro.

The way you generate topspin is by brushing up on the ball while bringing the racquet across the body.

GAINING CONFIDENCE WITH TOPSPIN

The emphasis when learning with the Wegner Method is control. By starting with slow, controlled strokes, you will learn the relationship between your swing and your shot's velocity, placement, and spin. You can

- Have a friend feed you one ball to your forehand and then one to your two-handed backhand, over and over. (Ideally, you'd ask the best player you could find to hit slowly and accurately, without making you run too much.) Start halfway between the baseline and the service line. As you become more proficient, continue to move back slightly until you're at the baseline. Hit the ball back and forth. Take your time, tracking the ball (especially after the bounce), finding it well, and emphasizing the finish.

    On both the forehand and backhand, at the finish, keep your racquet over your shoulder for an instant, reinforcing the relationship between the finish and your placement of the ball. Keep the ball in play at a slow enough pace so you can still find the ball easily and return it with a full and controlled stroke. Slowly build up your racquet speed as you find yourself able to handle more ball speed and movement on the court. Remember to accelerate from the contact point onward as you did with your forehand. Beware of rushing your stroke. If the other player hits a harder ball, refrain from hurrying and preparing too early.

    With the type of stroke you are learning, you can still watch the bounce, wait for the ball to get near you, find it, and finish. The faster you move your racquet forward, the farther away from you your contact point will be, thus lessening your control of the ball. To prevent this, wait a tiny bit longer if you want to hit hard. Pause increasingly longer the harder you want to hit. •

OPEN YOUR TWO-HANDED BACKHAND

A new development in the modern game is facing the net on the two-handed backhand, mirroring the open stance of the forehand. Although not yet a universal practice, some of the top pros have demonstrated the superiority of this technique.

First, landing on the outside foot (the left foot for a right-hander) provides much more support to come across powerfully through the ball, generating ball speed with the weight of the body. Shifting from the left foot to the right foot in such a natural way powers the shot surprisingly well.

Second, the two-handed backhand hit in an open stance makes it easier to recover toward the center after the hit, minimizing the time and effort involved. Rather than having to reposition the feet to move back to the center, you just lean in that direction and a simple pivot has you facing back toward the center so you can continue to cover the whole court.

Above all, the open stance keeps your hands closer to the ball, without having to reach across your body. This factor alone makes for an easier, more accurate shot, regardless of the speed of your opponent's shot. ●

experiment, but be careful not to stray too far from the essence of this technique. Playing too wildly at this stage or practicing with a player who returns the ball wildly can result in confused strokes. The goal is consistency in making your shots. You'll build confidence by hitting the same shot over and over and knowing where it landed each time. It is important that you realize you made each shot with a specific movement, a specific technique. There are a million ways to strike the ball, but very few of them are really effective.

You'll notice the idea of power is absent from the early learning stages in the Wegner Method. Stay focused on feel and control. Once you've mastered these skills, power can gradually come into your game, and you can stroke harder with confidence and control. By adding more and more topspin, you will eventually hit harder and harder and still make the ball drop into the opposite court. Just make sure you're not overwhelming your learning partner, and that he or she isn't overwhelming you.

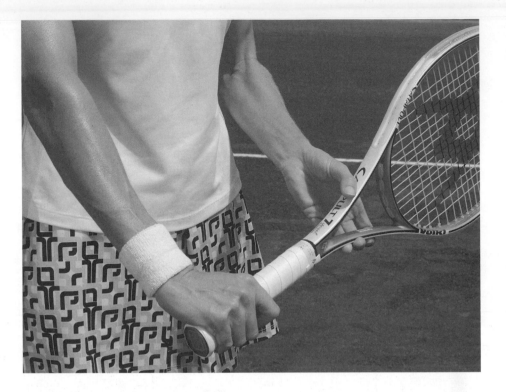

Bring the racquet parallel to your body, and your hand perpendicular to the handle (grip).

The One-Handed Backhand

Many players prefer all shots be one-handed. For the right-hander, this could result in an unbalanced use of the body, not giving as much exercise to the upper left side. If you want to play tennis in a more balanced way, try the two-handed backhand to exercise both sides of the upper body.

However, if you feel, like me, that you will perform better hitting backhands only with your right hand, here's how to make them strong and accurate.

THE ONE-HANDED BACKHAND GRIP

Hold the racquet with your left hand at the throat, your right hand on the grip, and your right thumb behind the grip—as if pasting a stamp on a letter with your thumb (see photo above).

Notice the player in this photo has let her arms down, with the racquet head at a right angle to both arms and parallel to the front of her body.

THE ONE-HANDED BACKHAND 1-2-3-4

The backhand has four easy steps:

1. Stand in the ready position in the center of the court with the racquet butt against your navel. Hold the racquet with your forehand grip.
2. Pivot and move to the ball naturally, changing your grip to the backhand grip as you turn to the left, as shown in the photo opposite. Move to intercept the ball while pointing the butt of the racquet toward it.
3. Still facing sideways, find the ball by extending your arm slowly to the right until your racquet is parallel to the net. Meet the ball well to your right and slightly below the center of the strings.

The ready position (left).

Point to the ball with the butt of the racquet (right).

Meet the ball to your right (left).

Follow through upward (right).

4. Accelerate your arm up and across to your right, finishing with your arm at or well above shoulder level and your racquet pointing straight up. The left arm stays down and moves farther back, bringing the shoulder blades close to each other.

The left-handed one-handed backhand uses the same steps, but the directions are reversed:

1. Stand in the ready position in the center of the court with the racquet

Point to the ball with the butt of the racquet.

Meet the ball to your left (left).

Follow through upward (right).

butt against your navel. Hold the racquet with your forehand grip.

2. Pivot and move to the ball naturally, changing your grip to the backhand grip as you turn to the right, as shown in the bottom photo on page 116. Move to intercept the ball while pointing the butt of the racquet toward it.

3. Still facing sideways, find the ball by extending your arm slowly to the left until your racquet is parallel to the net. Meet the ball well to your left and slightly below the center of the strings.

4. Accelerate your arm up and across to your left, finishing with your arm at or well above shoulder level and your racquet pointing straight up. The right arm stays down and moves farther back, bringing the shoulder blades close to each other.

Thumb position.

- Practice the one-handed backhand motions without a racquet until you have the motions down fluidly. Repeat with your eyes closed to increase your feel of the motion.
- Put your right thumb behind the strings. Turn sideways to the net, bringing your racquet parallel to your body and steadying the racquet with your left hand. Have a friend slowly toss the ball a foot to your left side, so it hits the ground 3 or 4 feet in front of you and bounces to waist height. Using this shortened grip, execute the backhand, lifting your arm above your shoulder. After your swing, leave the arm up at the finish for a couple of seconds to solidify the relationship between your finish and the placement of your shot in your opponent's court. Repeat, gradually moving your thumb onto the grip to lengthen the racquet. Keep practicing until you are consistently connecting with the ball and placing it successfully where you want

The starting position.

it. Now have your friend throw the ball farther out from your left side. Increase your focus on the finish by bringing your left arm back for balance, feeling your shoulder blades moving close to each other. By focusing on the finish, you lose any tightness from overattention on how to hit the ball, and you train your arm to lift pronouncedly. When comfortable with the movement, move your hand to the normal grip position and exaggerate the finish. See photos opposite and this page. ●

As you progress, move your grip gradually toward the racquet grip.

When you are confident, move your hand all the way to the end of the grip, while your left hand steadies the racquet from the throat.

Always finish high, squeezing your shoulder blades.

While you don't want to overfocus your attention on your footwork, you still need to become comfortable with the instinctive motions your body makes as you move toward a ball on your left.

Maintain the backhand grip all the time to familiarize yourself with it. You will probably make slight adjustments in your grip and swing as you develop a better feel for the one-handed backhand and the most efficient swing possible. As long as you are clearing the net safely and have the ball speed under control, keep lifting away. Your upper back muscles will become stronger with time, so do not overdo your first practice day, or you may become sore.

- Place a can of balls a few feet in front of the baseline in the center of the court. Stand in front of the can, holding the racquet in the one-handed backhand grip. Turn to your left and start walking, looking to your right at your friend, who is ready to toss the ball toward your

On this drill, keep your arm extended and use a one-handed backhand grip at all times (left).

Turn and walk naturally, pointing the butt of the racquet to the incoming ball (right).

Find the ball to your right, slightly below the center of the strings (left).

Exaggerate the finish, up and toward your right (right).

backhand side. Have your friend toss the ball slightly in front of you, making sure it bounces well before it reaches you and that you have time and room to adjust. Find the ball toward the right side of your body, your right arm fully extended. As you touch the ball, accelerate your arm upward to lift the ball over the net. Finish with your right arm fully extended toward the net and your left arm extended down and backward to maintain your balance. After finishing your swing, turn to your right, keeping the racquet up as you walk back toward the center of the court. Watch where your shot lands to reinforce the finish while feeling your shoulder blades close together. To keep the ball and your opponent in sight, avoid turning your back to your opponent's court. See photos pages 120–22.

After you hit a backhand, always turn to your right, and when you reach the center of the court, turn to your left to face the net. Walk counterclockwise behind the can of balls while bringing your racquet down.

With the racquet still up to reinforce the finish, turn toward the center (left).

Still holding the backhand grip, go around the can from the backcourt and repeat the drill (right).

Turn toward the net and go for the next ball. Practice until you're consistently connecting with the ball and placing it where you want it. Now gradually move the can toward the baseline. You can leave your thumb against the back side of the grip, or you can drop it all the way around the grip. As players become very good, they usually end up with the thumb down and around the grip, which makes it easier to adjust the racquet to low balls. ●

- Hit back and forth with someone returning the ball only to your backhand at a slow pace. You don't have to return all the way to the centerline after each shot but can remain comfortably on your backhand side of the court, turning to the right after you finish the stroke, then to the left again for the next ball. Keep practicing until you feel sure of the connection between your full finish and your placement of the ball, and you can rally twenty to thirty times without missing. This may take more than one session to accomplish. Listen to your body's signals about when it is time to stop. Overtired muscles lead to poorly controlled strokes and possibly even pain. •

BUILDING A TOPSPIN BACKHAND

To improve your topspin backhand, hold your racquet in your backhand grip. Stand sideways to the tennis court fence, an arm's length away from the fence, with your arm pointing to the fence. The racquet and your knuckles should touch the fence. Keep the racquet and arm perpendicular to each other—your arm pointing to the fence and your racquet parallel to it. If you need support for the racquet, you can put your thumb behind the grip.

First, press the racquet into the fence, with the head of the racquet slightly lower than your fist. Then move a couple of inches away to prevent your knuckles from hitting the fence. Bring the racquet to your front with the butt pointing to the fence. Then bring your racquet slowly to the fence with your arm extended, and then rapidly swing across the surface of the fence without hitting or touching it. Lift your arm and rotate the racquet upward in a windshield wiper motion, as if brushing the fence.

As you swing, your body can help this motion by lifting your trunk, moving it backward, and pulling your shoulder blades together. Try each of these (lifting, moving, pulling) separately, and then try them in different combinations. Choose the combination that feels best to you. The top pros usually combine all three to help the arm and the stroke.

After you have this movement well grooved into your body, go on the court and have someone toss balls gently to your backhand. Lift the ball well over the net and finish all the way, perhaps exaggerating the lift and the finish even further. Maintain your balance by pulling away from the ball and up, especially if you are too close to the ball. Pulling back provides plenty of room to swing, with your arm extending toward the target and then across your body toward the right. Note that you bend your arm pronouncedly on the topspin forehand, while on the one-handed topspin backhand, your arm extends—straightens—as far as it will go. This technique involves the larger muscles in your upper back.

Gradually, let the ball come closer to you. This forces you to lift your body and back up, accelerating your racquet in a much more pronounced way, thus increasing the speed of your shot. This back-and-up movement combination has been shunned by conventional tennis teaching (which tells you to step forward into the hit and stay down). This, unfortunately, destroys the natural acceleration of the arm. Try it both ways—the conventional way and the Wegner Method—and you'll notice the difference. •

The Backhand Slice

The backhand slice, whether one-handed or two-handed, is a backhand shot hit from high to low with the racquet face opened sharply. It is similar to the backhand volley, except that you accelerate from the ball onward, continuing well past the contact with the ball, while with the volley, you stop as you hit.

By hitting down and leading the stroke with the bottom edge of the racquet, you brush underneath the ball and make it spin backward. This is the opposite of topspin and is called *underspin* or *slice*. This spin creates more air friction at the bottom of the ball than on the top, keeping it in the air longer. The ball tends to hang in the air longer than the pronounced downward curve of topspin shots.

Sliced ground stokes have to be hit lower, with smaller clearances over the net than topspin shots, or they will go out-of-bounds. Professionals with one-handed backhands usually return fast serves with the sliced backhand because it can be shortened, blocking the return efficiently while still producing ball speed and accuracy.

If the serve comes to your forehand, it is a different story, because you can hit a forehand hard with topspin without the need for preparation. A very hard return will give your opponent trouble even when it doesn't go very deep. The same principle holds true for the two-handed backhand, which doesn't need any preparation prior to the hit. You jump at that fast serve and follow through hard, up and over the ball.

On the one-handed backhand return, you need more preparation, such as a shoulder turn and a backhand grip, to drive through the ball. A top pro may wait for the first serve favoring his one-handed backhand side, ready to slam a hard, flat or topspin backhand return. But this backhand return is a risky shot that requires tremendous skill and precision. You can't muscle the ball as well as with your forehand or a two-handed backhand. If you are a beginning or intermediate one-handed player, your safest choice for a booming first serve coming to your backhand is a blocked slice return. While rallying, a slice backhand hit firmly can give your opponent trouble by skidding and staying low.

You may prefer one style of backhand over another. If you feel that you can do better with just one type of stroke, I wouldn't disturb that feeling. Your confidence depends on what *you* feel about your game, not what others think about it. On the other hand, adding this slice stroke to your repertoire will make you a more complete player, helping you vary your strokes when needed, mixing slices with topspin strokes.

Personally, I consider this backhand easy and effective. I not only hit down on the slice, but also across to the right, squeezing my shoulder blades together.

Open the racquet face and use a backhand grip, with the fingers spread slightly apart.

Learning this stroke is easy. To start, you only have to point the butt of the racquet at the incoming ball to be ready. The racquet face stays open, as shown in the photo on page 125.

This will automatically change your grip to the backhand. The grip change doesn't need to be as pronounced as for the topspin backhand, as your fingers remain spread apart, similar to the forehand grip. The main change occurs at the bottom of the hand, which mounts the top bevel of the racquet grip. The best way to make this grip change is to pull from the throat of the racquet with the left hand while pointing the butt of the racquet to the ball. This brings the racquet to a position closer to perpendicular with your right forearm. Pulling the racquet with your left hand toward your left side is all the backswing you need for returning a fast ball. You'll be able to block the ball instinctively with a short stroke.

In the beginning, it is a good idea to point both the butt of the racquet and your elbow to the incoming ball while still holding the racquet with both hands. Then straighten your right arm at the elbow and separate the arms, squeezing your shoulder blades together. The left arm should stretch back to keep your balance and to prevent you from turning too early to your right, thus misdirecting the shot. See photos below.

The height of your shot will depend on how much your racquet face is open. While learning, keep the racquet face angle quite open and hit

Point the butt of the racquet to the incoming ball. Keep pointing it after the bounce (left).

At the last possible moment, meet the ball with a downward stroke. The face of the racquet is slightly open (middle).

Open both arms, hitting across the line (or trajectory) of the ball (right).

A PROFESSIONAL BACKHAND SLICE

The best way to control a backhand slice is to cock your wrist as if you were look-ing at a ring on your middle finger. This could be part of tracking the ball, cocking the wrist at the same time that you point the butt of the racquet at the incoming ball.

You need to perfect this racquet-butt alignment after the bounce, tracking the ball with it as long as possible, and letting the ball onto your racquet, rather than chasing the ball with the racquet's head. As the ball is nearing you, follow it with the butt of the racquet, and let the ball cross over your hand and into your racquet's head.

At that point you "push" it, moving the butt of the racquet forward (toward the net) and then sharply across, squeezing your shoulder blades together. Aid this motion by lifting your trunk.

Find the ball well first, making sure your elbow is far enough from your body to allow your arm free motion across the ball. Strike firmly at the last possible mo-ment, using your back muscles to pull your arms back even farther, bringing your shoulder blades together as you strike.

The ball speed attained with this type of stroke is amazing. The ball stays low and has "bite." Your hand and racquet are not only moving across the body, but across the line of the ball as well. ●

down on the ball. Make it very different from your topspin stroke, so you do not confuse them.

If you have a two-handed backhand and also want to slice the ball using both hands, simply open the racquet face, find the ball well, and hit from high to low. Practice will tell you all the refinements as to rac-quet angle and spin. There are no complications or secrets. On your top-spin, close the racquet face and hit up. On your slice, open the racquet face and hit down.

Some of the top pros have a two-handed topspin backhand but use a one-handed backhand slice. You can emulate them by pulling from the throat of the racquet with your left hand as you turn to your left, push-ing away with your right hand, and pointing the butt of the racquet to the incoming ball. This will automatically bring about the backhand-slice grip in your right hand while imparting greater firmness to your stroke than would result from maintaining the forehand grip.

Even if you are strictly a two-hander in your backhand, you should practice the one-handed slice. In some situations it is very difficult or even impossible to reach the ball with both hands on the racquet. If you have practiced a one-handed backhand slice, you'll instinctively reach for the ball that way and possibly keep the ball in play, saving you from a certain point loss.

Changing Grips

If you use a one-handed backhand, you'll need to develop a smooth, fluid transition between your forehand and backhand grips. Your left hand can help by pulling back at the throat of the racquet, which allows the grip to slide down slightly inside your right hand. You can set your thumb behind the racquet or keep your fingers close together, whichever feels more comfortable and natural at this point for the one-handed backhand grip. One-handed backhand grips are usually tighter throughout the stroke than forehand grips where you can relax the hand much more. As a further subtlety, many professionals turn their right shoulder toward the ball in the backhand. Just be sure you find the ball with your hand and racquet and not with your shoulder.

Start with the forehand grip.

Then change to the backhand grip.

To practice changing grips, start with the forehand grip (see photo opposite). Put the racquet butt against your navel, perpendicular to the body. Your left hand steadies and balances the racquet in the basic ready position.

To change to the backhand grip, straighten your right arm, setting your right thumb behind the grip, with the racquet parallel to the body (see photo above).

- Change from your forehand grip to the one-handed backhand grip without looking at the racquet until you can do so smoothly. Repeat with your eyes closed to feel the two positions and the transition between them.
- Practice swinging at an imaginary ball, alternating between forehand and backhand strokes, until you are comfortable switching to the proper grip. Emphasize the finish.
- Stand in the center of the court behind the service line, facing the net in the ready position. First, have your friend feed a ball to your forehand side and hit a forehand. Turn to your left, leaving the racquet over your shoulder until you see the ball bounce in your opponent's court. As you walk past the centerline, change to your backhand grip, pointing the butt of the racquet toward the ball in your friend's hand. Have

your friend feed a ball to your backhand side and hit a backhand. Leave the racquet up while you turn to your right, again watching where you placed your shot as you return to the centerline. Change to your forehand grip while still walking to your right, returning the racquet butt to your navel. Your friend continues alternating balls to your forehand and backhand sides as you practice changing grips until you feel your hand sliding naturally into the proper grip for each particular stroke. Do not look at your hands while changing from forehand to backhand. Feel the grip to find it.

- If you are having trouble shifting from one grip to the other, take a few minutes to practice this grip-change sequence with your eyes closed: Face the net in the ready position using your forehand grip. Turn your shoulders to your left while pulling back from the racquet throat with your left hand. At the same time, point the racquet butt to an imaginary ball coming to your backhand side. Slightly loosen your right-hand grip while sliding your thumb behind the grip. Tighten your right-hand grip again. Set your arms and shoulders as if preparing for a backhand stroke. Then face the net again, centering your racquet in your forehand grip at the ready position. This sequence, although broken down here for ease of understanding, in practice is a continuous, smooth motion. Keep it simple and drill until you feel the grip changes are fluid but exact. Again, don't watch your hands.

- Now rally back and forth with a player who controls the ball using forehands and one-handed backhands. Maintain a slow pace. The balls should not be too far from your reach. Stand halfway between the service line and the baseline in the center of the court. Hit the ball 2 to 3 feet over the net and stroke gently and upward. Both players should play deliberately, with slow but fully finished strokes, and not rush their shots. This is not yet a game. You are still developing your strokes and want to keep the same feel, control, and finish in each stroke. The slower you do things at this stage, the more efficient you will become, allowing you to make easier adjustments to faster balls later. If you lose either the feel of your swing or your confidence, they will return if you find the ball well and emphasize the finish of your swing. Or go back to earlier drills, choosing the ones that apply to the stroke in question, and practice them until you are confident and comfortable with all your strokes. •

SIMPLICITY

What is the strength that separates the very top pros from the rest of the field? Is it technique, focus, mental strength, tactics, or all of the above? You could call it a combination of all of these, but in a special way.

Strangely enough, these aspects are interrelated, geared to help each other in simplifying the task of handling the ball. The body helps the stroke, the focus helps the mind, the timing helps the control and power. The tactics capitalize on your strengths.

Let's say you are a player well taught by conventional teaching standards, and you are playing in a tournament. You pay attention to your foot position and the path of your backswing. You make sure to prepare early for the shot (you've already pictured in your mind where the ball is going to bounce and how). And you are thinking where you are going to hit the shot to make sure you don't miss it and to force your opponent to run. What will happen? You'll probably miss the ball entirely!

Top pros achieve a delicate balance of timing, power, control, coordination, focus, and endurance with extreme simplicity. They've trimmed away the complexities. Most of the top pros today had a role model when they were young, a player they admired as a performer for his or her strokes, and whom they imitated.

The Williams sisters broke this copy-cat start, and they set new standards. How did this happen? According to their father Richard, they watched my televised lessons in the early 1990s. Although my instruction portrayed unconventional tennis teaching, he told me: "It made sense."

Among Venus's and Serena's "firsts" was the open-stance, two-handed backhand, a fabulous shot at which both excel. Their forehands were also opposed to the most commonly enforced forehand tenets of conventional coaching; they both hit open stance and over the left shoulder.

To sum it up, the best technique and the best way of performing are the simplest of all. Years ago, after a three-hour U.S. Open match (which he won), Pete Sampras was asked what he thought about during the match. He considered the question and replied, "I think I had one thought," meaning that his mind had been mostly blank throughout the entire game. This is what top players call being "in the zone."

So simplify your tennis, feel the ball on your strings, and avoid thinking of anything else but the ball.

If you have trouble clearing your mind, count silently to 5: "1" at the bounce, then "2," "3," "4," perhaps a little pause, and then hit at "5." At first, it may seem impossible. But I have tested it with beginners, advanced players, and pros. They all found it very helpful and also concurred that it helped slow down their minds.   •

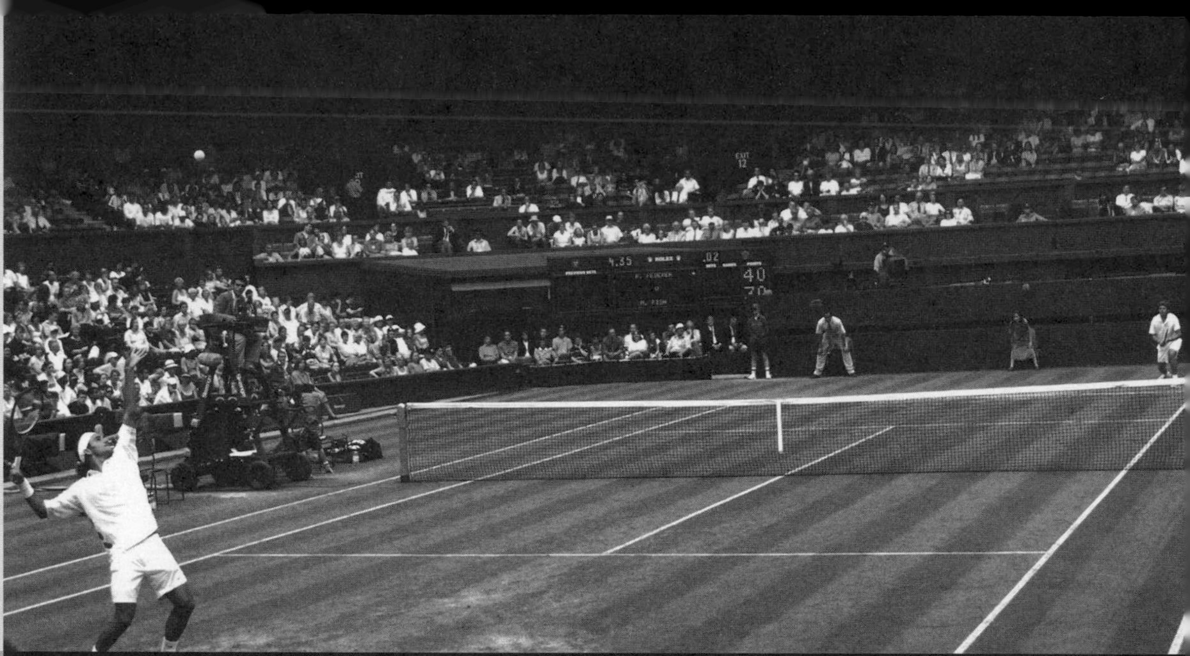

6 the serve

Roger Federer serves to Andy Roddick. [Art Seitz]

WHEN YOU PLAY GAMES and count points—instead of just rallying back and forth—the *serve* or *service* puts the ball into play. Standing behind the baseline, you serve the ball into your opponent's court. You serve the first point from the right side of the court, hitting the ball to your left into the opposite service court (see top illustration opposite).

You serve the second point from the left side, again hitting the ball diagonally into the opposite service court. You have two chances to hit a good serve on each point. If both miss, you lose the point, which is called a *double fault*. After each point, you alternate between serving from your right court and your left court (see bottom illustration).

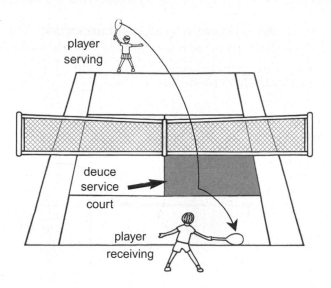

The first serve is always hit into your opponent's right-hand service area, called the deuce service court.

You are not allowed to touch the baseline or the inside of the court with your foot as you serve (called a *foot fault*). Your foot can land inside the court or on the baseline only after the ball leaves your racquet.

The server has the choice of serving either underhand or overhead, as long as the ball is hit before it bounces after the toss. Pro and good club players serve overhead because the height of the contact point with the ball gives a better angle for the shot and lets them hit with more force. Advanced players also use spin during the serve to make the ball curve down, sideways, or both. As you progress, your serve, perhaps more than any other stroke, will become unique to you, since it tends to have more variation in personal style and technique than other strokes.

Serves are not hard to learn. For the overhead serve, toss the ball up with your left hand and swing overhead to connect with the ball as it comes back down. Some simple drills will help you master this stroke. *Note:* Before you try harder serves, be sure you end your swing consistently with your right arm moving down across your body and to your

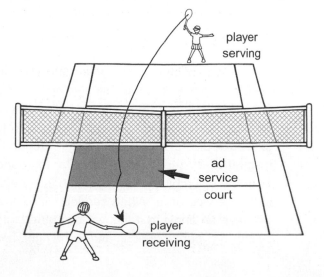

The second serve is hit into your opponent's left-hand service area, called the ad service court (*ad* is short for *advantage*).

left to avoid hitting your legs with the racquet. This should be no problem in the beginning because your swing should be smooth and slow. When your arm passes below your waist, bring your right hand toward your left hip, finishing with the racquet throat in your left hand.

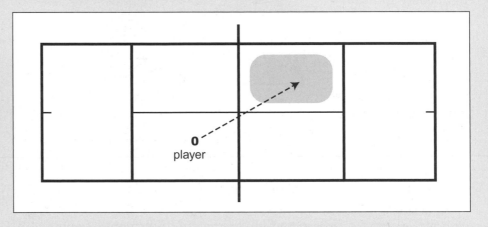

Start the service drill close to the net.

- Stand about 6 feet from the net, to the right of the centerline. Without your racquet, make a gentle overhead throw over the net to land the ball in the correct service court (the one diagonally across the net) (see top photos opposite). Repeat several times and observe how the ball curves down into the service court.
- Now pick up your racquet at the throat with your regular forehand grip so you're choking up on the racquet, holding the racquet the way you would a hammer (called a **hammer grip**) (see bottom photo opposite). Hold the ball (either a regular tennis ball or a larger practice ball) in your left hand, with your hands slightly above your face. Toss the ball above your racquet strings, and with your racquet slightly open (see photos page 136), push the ball gently over the net and into the service court (see left photo page 137). This push comes from extending your arm toward your target. Depending on the angle of your racquet when serving with a regular forehand grip, you may need to push the ball a bit to the right of the intended target in order to land it in the service area. When serving with a hammer grip, the racquet will have an angle to it that will send the ball to the left. Compensate by moving your racquet up and to the right, and the ball will go into the

Toss the ball overhead toward the service court (left).

Follow through with your whole arm (right).

Start with the racquet short in a hammer grip.

Toss the ball above your racquet (left).

Meet the ball with the racquet slightly opened (right).

service court. Finish the stroke by continuing the racquet motion down and across the front of your body (see right photo). Serve balls from this position near the net and choked up on the racquet until you are successful in consistently placing the ball in the correct court. Always move your hand forward, rather than just the racquet head.

- Have a bucket of balls ready. Gently hit serves into the correct service court. Every time you place the ball in the service court, move one step back toward the baseline, staying to the right of the centerline. Every time you miss a serve, take a step forward toward the net. (If you swing at the ball and miss it entirely, it still counts, so take a step forward.) As you move away from the net, you can move your hand gradually toward the normal grip position, or you can keep the racquet "short" for a while. Do what feels best to develop your serve at your own speed. Either way, stretch your arm upward so that your contact point is high and you can hit the ball over the net. The combination of the angle of your racquet face and the direction of your swing determines whether the ball goes toward the left, right, or center. By moving

Push the ball over the net gently (left).

Finish on your left side, with the throat of the racquet in your left hand (right).

If the ball touches the top of the net and lands in the correct service court, repeat the serve from the same position. This is called a **let**, from the Old English **lettan**, meaning **to hinder**, because the net has hindered the other player from returning the serve normally. A let can make it too hard for the player returning the ball to hit it, so the rule is that, if there is a let, you repeat your serve from the same side of the court. If the ball touches the net and bounces out of your opponent's service court, the serve is a miss.

away from the net only after a successful serve, you'll instinctively focus on control as you put the serve into the right box. You will learn how much power you need to release to place the ball over the net and still drop it into the service court. See illustration below and photos next page.

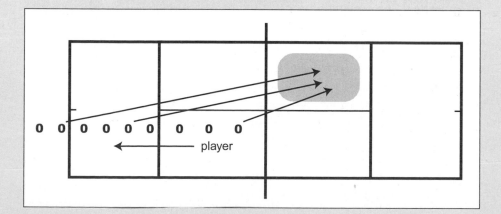

player

The drill sequence.

From farther back, swing faster and clear the net by 2 or 3 feet (left).

From behind the baseline, swing freely but with control (right).

- Come close to the net again, this time standing to the left of the centerline. You'll be serving to the service court across the net and to your right. Repeat the same drill sequence that you did on the right side of your court: one step back toward the baseline for every serve you hit in, and one step forward for every serve that lands outside the service court. When you reach the baseline, keep moving back one step at a time until you are about 6 feet behind the baseline. See photos opposite. This extra distance will lengthen your swing. You're doing this only as a drill. Normally, you'll stand just behind the baseline for game serves. To achieve more power, you may also want to start with a slightly closed stance (sideways to the net), as if throwing something a far distance. Your toss may be a little higher and your swing a little longer. Let your toss and swing develop as you practice hitting the ball over the net and into each service court.

- Stand behind the baseline to the right of the centerline and start serving from there. When you can hit the ball consistently into the proper service court, switch to the left side and repeat.

- To add spin, approach the ball using the front edge of your racquet. Hold the racquet in a hammer grip, choking up on the racquet slightly to shorten it if you like. Raise both arms, keeping the edge of the racquet forward. Toss the ball above your head with your left arm while the racquet drops behind your head. Swing up and across to your right as far as you can while twisting your arm and racquet to the right of the court. You are moving your arm and racquet across the ball from left to right as you serve, giving the ball a diagonal spin. This makes the ball curve in flight and kick higher after the bounce. Let the racquet drop down and

From the left side, swing a bit more to the right but finish by your left hip.

From the baseline, hit the ball even farther so it clears the net by a couple of feet or more.

To learn to spin the ball, address the ball with the racquet's edge.

Swing up and toward the right, spinning the ball.

across your body toward your left hip, and grab the racquet in your left hand in preparation for the next shot. The pros do it the same way. See photos this page and opposite.

• Serve a ball from the right side. You have two chances. If you hit it into the correct service court, count it as your point, then serve from the left side. If you missed the first serve, go for your second. If you succeed, count it as your point. If not, count it as your opponent's point. Repeat, serving from the left side. Alternate serving from the right and the left sides of the court for 10 to 20 points, or until you no longer serve any double faults. Double faults should be a rare thing, even at this stage. Next switch to your opponent's end of the court and serve 10 to 20 points. This is the basic learning process for your serve. You can do all this by yourself with a bucket of balls. Many professionals go out on the court to practice dozens of serves. Once you have developed your arm and shoulder muscles, you can do the same to learn and develop your serve. If you don't have many balls to do these drills, serve gently and have a friend catch your serves on the other side and throw the balls back to you (or if your friend is proficient, have him or her hit the ball to return the serves). Catch the ball and try another serve. ●

Let the racquet go down and across your front, catching it with your left hand.

Ready to serve (left).

The toss (right).

If you're left-handed, perform the same drills as above, but reverse the directions. See the photos above and opposite for what your full serve would look like.

POWERING UP YOUR SERVE

Most players would love to have more power in their serves. The strongest professional serves have considerable topspin ball rotation. The following two drills will strengthen your serve while developing control from ball rotation.

The first drill develops the feel of bending and extending the arm, using the triceps as the main driving muscle. Most people depend too much on the shorter and weaker shoulder muscles for serving, which causes most serving injuries. Using the triceps as the major force behind the serve is a better choice. As you do this drill, you will notice at first that you don't hit up as much as you think you do. Even professionals, when doing this drill, often hit the ball into the fence at first.

Note that in the second drill, regardless of how you try to hit the ball, your serve will tend to have a good amount of spin as a natural consequence of the upward

The contact (left).

The finish (right).

movement of your arm, emphasized while hitting the ball over the fence. Even when you serve hard, you'll notice a fair amount of spin. This combination of ball speed and spin is ideal for developing a strong first serve. (Bear in mind that top pros have considerable spin on the first serve, sometimes exceeding 3,000 rpm.)

The combination of these drills, even if done only once each, will give you a much stronger serve. Just be careful not to strain your arm and overdo it by hitting too hard or hitting too many balls. Be aware of how you feel and use common sense to determine how far and how hard you can go.

1. Go outside a fenced-in court. Standing about 30 to 35 feet away, spin a good number of balls over the back fence.
2. When you are consistently and comfortably hitting over the fence, return to the court and hit from the normal service position. You may need to

adjust the angle of your wrist, as if you were looking into the palm of your hand; otherwise, the ball may be too high and not drop into the service court. To maintain the spin, swing across to your right (for a right-hander), then finish with the racquet on your left hand.

3. Stand in a large area such as a field and try serving balls as far as you can. This develops the natural release you have when throwing any kind of object. When you return to the court, you'll need to adjust your wrist position as mentioned above. ●

SECOND-SERVE SPIN

One of the most important strokes in tennis is the second serve, which, to be safe, needs much more spin than your first serve.

It is better to first master the spin serve, then work on the harder and flatter first serve. The spin serve gives the ball a more pronounced downward curve than the flat stroke, allowing a larger clearance above the net. This provides a greater margin for error, giving the player the confidence to swing harder and higher above the net without worrying about the ball going past the service line. Most top pros excel in placing the second serve deep, with a high bounce of the ball that prevents the other player from taking the initiative early in the point. Some top players in the world have been known to hit second serves in excess of 5,000 rpm.

The hitting-over-the-fence drill developed an upward movement of your service stroke and some spin. Now you're ready to add more spin.

For a while, serve your first and second serves across the ball, generating plenty of spin, especially in practice, until you are totally confident your serve lands in the service area nearly all the time, no matter how hard you hit. Then you can risk flattening your first serve as much as you like. If you miss it, you still have a good second serve to rely on.

1. To test your spin on the court, serve the ball so it travels about 6 feet above the net. You'll see the ball starting upward and then curving down. If you have created enough spin, the ball will curve down into the serving box and then "kick" considerably as it bounces.

2. To exaggerate the kick, break your wrist inward (without changing your grip) so that the racquet is almost parallel to your chest. Toss the ball a bit behind you. As you swing up at the ball, the racquet travels almost parallel to and above the top of your head, and then it travels to the right as you hit the ball. Remember to address the ball with the racquet's front edge and to continue the swing upward and 2 to 4 feet toward the right before allowing the racquet to drop to your left. Even though your serving motion is moving toward your right, the angle of the racquet face makes the ball go straight forward toward the net. Lead the downward movement with the other edge of the racquet, letting it cross in front of your body and catching it with your left hand. With some practice, you will see greater and greater clearance over the net while the spin is still bringing the ball down in the service area, usually with good depth. •

Return of Serve

There are two distinct returns of serve. One is the response to a forceful serve in which you block the ball with the goal of sending it back into your opponent's court. The second is the reply to an easier serve whereby you drive the ball forcefully down the line, crosscourt, or down the middle.

For the blocked return, keep your racquet in front more than usual and bring your racquet to the ball with a short and firm back-and-forth action. Use the momentum of the incoming ball to develop good speed on your return ball.

You need to tighten your grip prior to the impact with the ball and to be very conscious of the angle of your racquet, because it will determine both the placement of your shot and whether the ball goes over the net. When returning a serve, the racquet face angle is usually fairly vertical. The stroke resembles a volley, except you hit from the ball forward with more of a follow-through.

Professional players make sure they place the return of serve in the court. If they have the opportunity to drive the return they will definitely do so, but their priority is to place the ball in the court, thereby pressuring the opponent. Balls constantly coming back to the server make him feel he has to be more forceful in his serves, and so he begins to make mistakes.

Players with forceful serves have the upper hand, winning points on serves their opponents cannot return. They also force their opponents to mis-time and mis-hit service returns, earning more outright service winners. These points won, added to the normal percentage of return errors and weak returns of serves that are easy to put away, give the player with a very good first serve a tremendous advantage.

On grass courts, it is unusual to see good serve-and-volley players lose their service game. The low and uneven bounce of the ball, especially when the grass is damp and slippery, makes returns and passing shots very difficult.

On hard courts, speeds vary according to the surface roughness, the paint mix used for coating the court, and whether it has a cement or asphalt base. If the court is hard, smooth, or slick, the game is very fast and that favors the big server. Some years ago in the United States, the tendency was to build very fast hard courts, especially for the major championships, thereby favoring the big serve-and-volley players. Today, most hard courts have surfaces that slow down play to the point where you can play successfully from the backcourt against a net rusher, although big serve-and-volley players still have an advantage on their service games.

On clay courts you have plenty of time to hit good returns of serve. Stand behind the baseline to return a hard first serve, using your normal strokes. If your opponent misses the first serve, move inside the baseline to return his second serve. The second serve will most likely be slower and shorter or else there is the risk of serving a double fault.

RETURNING A TWIST SERVE

Professionals rely on a twist second serve, called a *kick serve*, otherwise known as an *American Twist*, because of its accuracy and safety. They spin the ball so much, that even while clearing the net by 2 to 3 feet, the ball still curves down into the service court where it bounces quite high. A player facing a twist serve has two options: The easier one is to move

RETURN OF SERVE POINTERS

- Place your return of serve in the court, any way you can. Then you can really start the point.
- Finding the ball is a **must**. Most people think of their stroke first. Against a big serve, they are trained to react right away with the arm. On the contrary, avoid rushing your arm. React first with your body as a whole, find the ball with your racquet, then hit.
- You need to observe where the ball is going after the bounce in your service court, even if there seems to be no time, or you'll miss more returns than you make. React fast to a hard serve, but observe the ball as it closes in on you, and be fully aware of meeting the ball in the optimum area of your racquet strings.
- As you find the ball, refine your racquet angle to control your shot. There isn't much time when receiving a hard serve; however, instincts honed with practice will help you adjust your racquet, but only if you don't overreact.
- Send the ball safely over the net first. Then as you achieve greater accuracy and gain more experience, work on developing better angles and harder returns. ●

back so the ball loses some of its height and spin, and then drive it back with topspin. The other choice is to move forward to hit the ball before it rises above your shoulders. This second choice is risky because the ball has not yet lost its ball-rotation sting. However, a firmly blocked return should place the ball in your opponent's court.

Attacking the ball right after the bounce on a twist serve is a specialty of some top players. It requires perfect timing and a closed racquet angle to keep the ball from coming off the racquet higher than intended or off to either side of the court. Other pros stay back and resort to hitting the ball harder than it came into their racquet, thereby canceling the effect of these spinning balls. If there is any difficulty on a particular shot, they switch to a firmly blocked return.

If you are facing a twist player, it generally takes several service returns to understand what you have to do to block the ball with precision. Don't despair. Even the pros sometimes experience this at the beginning of a match but manage to adjust as the match progresses.

Many players have trouble adjusting to a left-handed player's serve because the ball curves and kicks differently. If you are right-handed and a left-hander is curving the ball to your backhand side, you need to move in diagonally to make a dent with your return. Otherwise, the ball will slip farther and farther away. The best option, prior to facing a lefty in a tournament match, is to practice with a left-handed player with such a serve.

how to return a hard ball

7

YOU MAY FIND that your opponent is trying to overwhelm you with power. The best way to handle this is to use the force of the incoming ball when you hit back. Just as with your other strokes, your goal is to reach the ball, find it well, accelerate the swing after contact, and make sure you finish properly.

The critical point is to track the ball, especially after the bounce, with your eyes, your racquet, and your hand. Forget about having the perfect position and about racquet preparation. Don't even think.

center

modern racquet
sweet spot

optimum contact point for
ground strokes

*Hitting the ball off-center
helps keep the racquet
closed.*

Just track the ball as if you were intending to stop it with your racquet—
then give it your usual hit.

You may lose some power by having the racquet approach the ball
slowly, but you'll be confident that your shot will stay in the court.
When you have this down well, then you can focus on building your
own power.

Some players, including many tennis teachers, may think this advice is too simple. So it's worth repeating: All you need to do is focus
on finding the ball while taking your time and finishing the stroke all
the way. You already learned this in the earlier chapters, but it is such a
key lesson, and a revolution in tennis teaching. So make sure you really grasp it!

The other critical factor in returning a hard ball is not to meet the
ball head on. Deflect it with the lower part of the strings. Just as in martial arts, you turn your opponent's force around and send it back in the
direction it came from.

What this means on ground strokes, especially on topspin strokes, is
that you direct the force not only up but also across the body, rather
than simply toward the intended target. The players who really make an
impact in major championship events invariably stroke across the body,
not toward the opposite court.

Returning with a Forehand

So how should you apply these ideas to your game? On your forehand, simply wrap the racquet across your body toward the left shoulder, in an open stance. In other words, bend your arm and pull it close to you as you finish the stroke, rather than away. Do you lose power doing this? Absolutely not. Does the ball go only to your left? No. You've already learned that the direction of the ball is more dependent on the angle of the racquet at contact than on the direction of your swing.

So what's the most efficient way to return a hard ball? Use your body to produce the most power with the least effort. Move your arm closer to your body as you hit, and the power in the contraction of your biceps and pectoral muscles will explode the ball away from you. Let's demonstrate this idea with an easy test. Extend your right arm and have a friend block the forward movement of your hand. With your arm extended, you'll notice how difficult it is to move your hand forward. Now grab your friend's hand with your right hand and pull him toward you—instant success. In this across-the-body action, you use muscles much stronger than those available when you keep your arm straight.

For two-handed backhands, use the same path across the body. The power of the contraction of the left biceps and pectorals, your motion uncoiling at the waist, and the torque you are applying to the racquet handle with both hands all combine to explode the ball away from you.

Notice also how natural it becomes to produce topspin. You generate ball rotation and force with a swing that moves both upward and across the body. This same technique also allows you to deflect the incoming ball force and propel the ball back over the net, thus using the other player's power to your advantage.

Roger Federer. [Art Seitz]

Returning with a Backhand

The same basic principle applies when you use a backhand to return a hard ball. On the one-handed backhand, the racquet moves across your body to the right and up. The large group of muscles in your upper back help lift your arm and bring the shoulder blades together. The left arm goes back not only for balance, but also to increase this contraction and to create an explosion of power.

Top pros hit both the one-handed and the two-handed backhand across the ball and to their right (for right-handers) rather than swinging forward, even while hitting *down the line* (close to the sidelines rather than across the court).

Gustavo Kuerten. [Art Seitz]

On the two-handed backhand return, mimic your forehand. Simply pull the racquet across your body toward the right shoulder. Find the ball and wrap your arms toward the right side.

Keep in mind that with today's racquets you don't need to hit with the center of the strings. New racquets respond much better with topspin hits closer to the bottom edge, giving you a better feel and helpful torque that keeps the racquet angle closed. If you hit toward the bottom of the strings, the racquet tends to remain closed. If you hit toward the top of the strings, the racquet tends to open. Therefore, when producing topspin with this upward movement, hitting with the bottom of the strings prevents the racquet from opening up and the ball from shooting up too high. This is true for both forehand and backhand topspin strokes, and is especially effective in the return of serve.

Overall, be aware that the most efficient way of playing is to use your opponent's force to your advantage, rather than meeting it head-on.

Eventually, as you become proficient with your ground strokes, you can move in front of the baseline for some returns, catching your opponent's ball early while it has more power, using the incoming ball speed to deflect it back quickly, and cutting your opponent's available time to respond. Timing is at a premium in these quick shots, so if you experience too many mis-hits, or the tactic isn't working, return to that area of the court where you are most comfortable returning the ball.

Serena Williams. [Art Seitz]

8

the volley

IN TENNIS, hitting the ball in midair before it bounces is a specialized stroke called a *volley*. The volley is often an offensive shot, hit before the ball bounces to cut your opponent's time to recover. You hit most volleys when you're standing between the service line and the net or right at the net, angling your racquet face to direct the shot left or right.

Your game isn't complete unless you know how to play in any part of the court. Otherwise, an accomplished player can easily exploit the weaknesses in your game.

Moving to the Net

Volleys can occur at any height. The most comfortable to execute are at torso level. The most difficult are low volleys (shin height). With the strokes you'll be learning in this chapter, you'll be able to hit any volley with some mastery.

If you open the racquet face while hitting down, the ball will clear the net and go forward at a good pace, making this an effective basic shot. You may notice some backspin in the ball as a result of hitting downward. This helps the ball bounce low on the other side, making it harder for your opponent to hit a decent shot.

Top pros tend to stop the racquet like a punch. This is in contrast to ground strokes, which require follow-through and a full finish. See photos pages 155–57.

For the ready position at the net, hold the racquet head up (left).

Stop the racquet after the hit (right).

The backhand volley is usually hit one-handed (left).

High volleys are hit down
and forward with a slightly
open racquet face (right).

Low volley balls are blocked
with a very open racquet
face (left).

Try to stop the forward
motion of your swing as
soon as the ball has slid
across the racquet face
(right).

You'll hit many volleys from above net level, where it is logical to hit with a downward stroke (left).

When the ball drops below the top of the net you can also achieve great results by hitting down and forward with your racquet—providing the racquet face is very open. Then stop your hand firmly on contacting the ball, as when an ax stops abruptly after hitting a log (right).

Forehand Volley

Just as with your other strokes, it's best to learn the forehand volley one step at a time. Make sure you are proficient at each skill before tackling the next. Hand-eye coordination is particularly critical in volleying. It is easy to miscalculate the contact point because you have less time to judge the flight of the ball.

Even players at the highest level of the game tend to overreact and imagine where the ball is going to be, instead of tracking it all the way into the racquet. Do not rush your volley. Learning to wait with your hand, even while you jump, will give you more time to track fast-moving balls.

Backspin is a backward rotation of the ball, which creates a higher air resistance on the bottom of the ball than on the top. The bottom has to push against the oncoming air while the top of the ball travels backward in the same direction as the oncoming air, reducing the friction between the top of the ball and the air.

The air resistance on the bottom of the ball pushes it upward, meaning the ball tends to stay longer in the air. It also tends to skid on the bounce. See illustration.

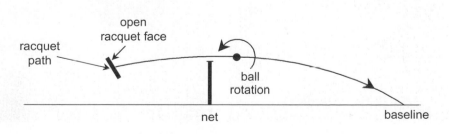

racquet path

open racquet face

ball rotation

net

baseline

In these drills, let the ball come near your racquet before you hit. Most volley errors are due to rushing the stroke. Instead, wait for the ball to come close and then block it firmly—slightly above the center on the top half of the racquet strings—making impact at your side or slightly in front of the body. Striking too early will decrease your ability to control the speed and direction of the ball.

It is more effective to keep the racquet face slightly open and to stroke down on the ball while swinging forward than to hit the ball forward with the racquet face flat or perpendicular to the ground. This slight downward brushing creates a backspin that lets you feel the ball longer and adds to your control.

Remember, angling the racquet to your right will send the ball right; angling the racquet to your left will send the ball left.

As you progress through these drills, gradually move your hand from the throat down toward the grip of the racquet, volleying 10 to 20 balls in each grip position. Don't rush these changes because it is easier to learn with the racquet gripped short than with your hand all the way down at the end of the grip.

Note that the left hand helps prepare the shot and lift the racquet when necessary. Let go of the racquet with your left hand prior to the hit but keep it in the vicinity of the racquet and come back to it after each hit.

- Stand in the center of the court, about 2 feet behind the net. Have a friend stand on the other side of the net, about 5 feet from it and slightly

Block the ball with your hand (left).

Block the ball with the racquet in front of your hand (right).

to your left. Have your friend toss a ball to your right side so that it comes to you at face height without bouncing. Block the ball downward firmly with your right hand so that it clears the net and goes down into your opponent's court (see left photo opposite). Stop the forward motion of your hand right after the moment of contact with the ball. Repeat until you can do this comfortably and consistently. Then change the angle of your hand slightly to send the ball in different directions. Keep doing this until you are successful with every hit.

• Hold your racquet with the right hand behind the strings and the left hand midway on the throat. Block the ball to volley as above, but keep your hand against the strings so that it still feels as if you are blocking the ball with your hand (see right photo opposite). Change the angle of the right hand and racquet to send the ball in different directions.

• Move your right hand to the throat of the racquet, with the tips of the fingers of your left hand on the throat, above the right hand. Block the ball downward with the racquet, sending the ball over the net and down into the other court (see photos below). Repeat until you have good control over the placement of your shots.

• Now move your hand into the normal grip, standing about 4 to 5 feet behind the net and volley from there. Your friend needs to stay to one side

Holding the racquet short, push the racquet back with your left hand, opening the racquet face (left).

With the racquet slightly opened, block the ball with the upper part of the string bed. Stop your hand and racquet right after contact (right).

The ready position, with a normal grip (left).

When you see the ball coming to your right, push the racquet head back (right).

Block the ball with a firm wrist.

to avoid being hit by your returns. Assume the ready position. Have your friend feed you some higher balls (only to your forehand side). As the ball comes toward you, tilt your racquet back, pushing with your left hand (see photos opposite). This will teach you to open the racquet face automatically, allowing you to hit down without hitting the ball into the net.

Open the racquet face for a low ball volley and move it slightly across toward your body.

- Next have your friend feed you some lower balls. Open your racquet face while you crouch to find the ball with your racquet (see photo this page). Lead the shot with the bottom edge of your racquet swinging downward, forward, and across toward your body. Stop after the ball leaves the racquet, keeping a firm wrist. The ball should rise and clear the net with space to spare. Try different racquet angles to determine how much to open your racquet for each shot. There isn't a set racquet angle. It all depends on how the ball is coming at you and how fast you want to hit it back. You want enough racquet angle to lift and clear the net, but not too much, or it will spin too much and be a slow shot.

- After you have the height and depth of these shots under control, have your friend stand in front of you and feed you some balls. Practice hitting forehand volleys, some to your friend's right and some to the left. To accomplish this, you only need to vary the angle of your racquet—right or left. You don't need to change your grip. Practice until the relationship between your racquet angle and where you place the ball becomes clear and then feels like second nature. •

FINE-TUNING
THE FOREHAND VOLLEY

One of the critical factors in the volley is timing. If you rush, you lose control of the shot. If you observe the top pros playing at the net (watching the player, not the ball), you'll notice that although they move early to approach the ball, the racquet hand waits for the ball to come near before they strike.

Take your time. If you prepare too much for the shot, you may miss the fact that there is so much time available. Being too busy, doing unnecessary things, can fill your time up so that it seems you need to hurry. If you feel rushed, silently count "1" when your opponent strikes the ball, then "2," "3," "4," and "5" when you hit.

Be economical. Extra movement only complicates your learning. To learn properly, do as little as you can. A good way to practice is to volley while standing still, so that you learn to adjust the hand instead of your whole body.

After you learn to adjust with your hand, have a friend feed you balls farther than your arm's reach. All top athletes in any sport lead a movement to the side with their head. Once the head—one of the heaviest parts of the body—leans beyond your outside foot, it starts your body in that direction. Very advanced players lift and drag the outside foot to accentuate the tilting of the body to bring about a quicker move. Once you are leaning, with your racquet still resting on both hands, your feet will push off in the most natural way, taking a jump. You will stretch to catch the ball with your racquet, touching it with the strings as you strike.

On the forehand side, make sure your elbow is tucked into the front of your body. A floating elbow causes plenty of errors and makes it more difficult to control the shot. When volleying a hard passing shot, your hand may make a short motion, like a punch, with practically no backswing at all, tightening up when you meet the ball. On a high and slow ball, your volley needs more follow-through, but again, always tighten your grip and your arm muscles when you meet the ball.

When executing ground strokes, it is best to get below the ball and hit up. The opposite is true with volleys: lift your racquet above the ball slightly, and hit down and across the ball, with an open racquet face, as if your racquet were going to the bottom of the net but with a very short punch.

Short, crosscourt volleys are most effective for winning points. If you are far from the net, volley deep to limit your opponent's options and keep moving forward. Then hit crosscourt at the first opportunity to put the ball away. If your opponent is anticipating this shot, hit behind him or her. This strategy works best when you bide your time instead of rushing your motions or decisions.   •

Backhand Volley

The most efficient net players hit all volleys with their dominant hand. They have a much greater reach hitting the backhand volley with one hand instead of keeping both hands on the racquet. If at any point you consider it necessary, you can assist a backhand volley with your left hand by keeping it on the racquet. This can help you avoid undue stress on your arm in the early stages of your tennis apprenticeship. As you do the drills in this section, you'll see that there is a lot of power in the one-handed backhand volley as well.

This power comes from the upper back muscles, rather than from your shoulders, if you properly align the racquet to the incoming ball. This is best done by pulling back with the left hand at the throat of the racquet while pushing forward with the right hand. This in effect points the butt of the racquet in the general direction of the incoming ball. At the same time the upper body helps by turning to the left.

24. MASTER THE BACKHAND VOLLEY

- If you have a soft training ball, practice blocking the ball with the back of your hand while standing sideways to the net (see top photo next page). Only use a soft practice ball because a regular tennis ball can hurt the back of your hand.
- Stand about 2 feet from the net and hold the racquet at the throat with your left hand as shown (see bottom left photo next page). Place the racquet in front of you, a little to your left about shoulder height. Place the back of your right hand behind the strings. Have your friend toss a ball toward your racquet. Block it downward into your opponent's court, keeping your hand against the strings. This gives you the feel of how hitting the backhand volley is like blocking it with the back of your hand.
- Grab the racquet by the grip with your right hand, placing your thumb against the back of the grip (see bottom right photo next page). Turn your shoulders and separate your elbow from your side. Pull the racquet back with your left hand while tracking the ball with the butt of the racquet. Turning the right shoulder sideways toward the net helps you hit

Mimicking the backhand volley with a soft training ball.

more comfortably, especially when you reach for a ball farther to your left (see top left photo opposite). Block the ball with the racquet face somewhat open. As you do, let go of the racquet with your left hand and move it backward (away from the grip, as if you were pulling back on a slingshot) just prior to the hit, while separating your arms. Always hit downward (see top right photo opposite). Feel your shoulder blades

With your right hand behind the strings, block the ball (left).

Use your thumb to support your grip (right).

squeezing together; at the moment of impact, stop the forward motion of your arm (see bottom photo). Move your hand not only forward but across to your right. After each hit, bring the racquet back up and onto your left hand.

- Have a friend stand in the other court (back far enough not to be hit by the return balls). Have him feed you some balls. Aim some volleys to his right and then to his left. Do this gently but firmly, varying the racquet angle but not your grip. Repeat until you have complete control of

Turn your shoulders and separate your right elbow from the body, tracking the ball with the butt of the racquet (left).

Hit downward with the racquet face slightly open (right).

Hit across the line of the ball and stop the racquet after impact.

your shot direction, and you meet every ball in the center or at the top half of your racquet strings. Now move your thumb down and around the grip (see top photo): the thumb against the back of the grip, although good for early stages, makes it difficult to open the racquet face for very low volleys. Practice volleying with this new grip. Make sure you can still volley firmly on high balls. If you have trouble with high volleys, keep your thumb against the back of the grip until you strengthen your hand and your arm.

As you progress, you may lower your thumb, but only if you are comfortable.

- Now move back a few more feet and volley from there until you have control. Have your friend feed you some higher balls. Point the butt of the racquet to the incoming ball and then block the ball firmly (see bottom photo). Lead the shot with the butt of your racquet, rather than with the racquet head and breaking the wrist. As you hit, extend the right arm toward the net and across to your right. The left arm extends down and behind you to help keep your balance. See top photos opposite.
- Next have your friend feed

Very high volley preparation.

Hit the ball while still high. Block the ball firmly (left).

Finish by stopping the racquet (right).

you low balls. Open the racquet face considerably and lead the shot with the bottom edge of your racquet, like a slicing action. Hit downward, forward toward the net, and also across (see bottom photo). Stop firmly just after contact with the ball, to send it over the net at a good pace. You'll notice this stroke doesn't feel like the "push" of your ground strokes with long finishes. You need to work out the correct angle of your racquet as you practice to ensure adequate speed and depth to your shot. If you undercut the ball too much, the shot

On low volleys, hit down and forward with a very open racquet face.

will be slow. Vary the angle of your racquet depending on the speed and height of the ball coming to you and the shot you want to hit. In the beginning, position the racquet face almost parallel to the ground to hit very low balls. Then start to adjust the angle according to the results. Racquet angling is learned from experience and instinct, not from being fixed in the same position all the time. •

PLAY LIKE THE PROS

FINE-TUNING THE BACKHAND VOLLEY

The notion that you can volley effectively without changing your grip at all between your forehand and backhand is somewhat inaccurate. Although many professionals volley without an apparent grip change between their forehand and backhand, there is nearly always some change at the heel of the hand.

On the forehand volley, the handle of the racquet is held slightly diagonally, while in the backhand volley, the racquet handle is held in the middle of the palm and somewhat perpendicular to it. This rotation is instinctive and born from practice, with the player adopting by feel the most efficient and powerful way to hit the ball.

For the best backhand volley, bring your hand across your body, slicing the ball rather than pushing forward. The stroke is short. Firm up your grip and your arm muscles at the impact with the ball. Make sure your elbow is away from your body and toward the ball, and that you hit across the body, at least to some extent. Advance the butt of the racquet across your body from left to right, as if elbowing something out of the way.

Keep the racquet face open, according to the height of the incoming shot. On the high volley, at the time of the impact, the racquet face will be somewhat perpendicular to the ground. With lower volleys, the racquet face should be dramatically open. Holding the elbow away from your body helps accentuate the opening of the racquet face.

Again, short, crosscourt volleys are the most effective for winning points. If you are far from the net, volley deep to limit your opponent's options and keep moving forward. Then hit crosscourt at the first opportunity to put the ball away. For right-handers, sharp and crosscourt backhand volleys are particularly effective against right-handed, one-handed backhand players, who generally have a weaker backhand than their forehand drive. •

Combining Forehand and Backhand Volleys

When you're waiting at the net for your opponent to hit the ball, hold the racquet in front of you, ready to move rapidly. Anticipate the direction of your opponent's next shot—to your right or left side—by carefully observing the racquet angle at the moment the racquet contacts the ball. As soon as you predict whether the ball is coming to your right or left, lean (move your head first) in that direction. Your upper body will automatically follow. Keep both hands on the racquet during this turn to adjust the grip between your forehand and backhand grips and line up your shot. Let go of the racquet with the left hand before the hit.

25. MASTER COMBINING FOREHAND AND BACKHAND VOLLEYS

In these drills, don't rush. Wait for the ball. Lean and turn slowly and deliberately, taking as much time as you can, instead of reaching out your racquet too fast. This way you'll move naturally. Going slowly also allows you to throw out any unnecessary movements that will trouble you at higher speeds. The slower you move at these slow ball speeds, simplifying your moves, the faster and more accurately you'll react to faster balls later.

Don't grip the racquet tightly between shots. Have the racquet rest on the fingertips of your left hand, holding the racquet head up. The right hand feels the grip, firmly but not tightly, with your body ready to react and find the ball with your racquet. Top pros make minimal grip changes at the net. These occur primarily at the base of the palm of the hand while reacting to the direction of the incoming ball. While you're learning, though, you'll probably want to change between your forehand and backhand grips to start you on the road to volleying. Later on, as you become more proficient at finding the ball at the net, you'll achieve more firmness and certainty in your contact with the ball. By then, you'll need less of a grip change in your volleys. Many players eventually adopt what's called the **continental grip**, halfway between a regular forehand and a one-handed backhand grip, similar to the way you'd hold a hammer but with the index finger slightly separated (see top photo).

The continental grip.

Some minor grip adjustments will occur naturally—even with a continental grip—for both forehand and backhand volleys to be truly efficient. Moving from the right to the left, and vice versa, the racquet position changes slightly in your hand.

By practicing these exercises, you'll learn to instinctively adjust your grip as needed. The best players volley firmly but not too hard. Hitting forcefully interferes with finding, feeling, and placing the ball.

Pull the racquet back with your left hand (left).

Release it from the left hand like a slingshot (right).

Push the racquet back with your left hand (left).

Block the ball firmly (right).

- Starting with slow balls, have your friend alternate tossing the ball to your right and left sides. After you start to move, release your left hand from the racquet as late as you can. Then hit, tightening up your arm through the contact with the ball to stop the racquet firmly. See photos opposite and this page. Return to the ready position by leaning and stepping back to where you came from, usually the centerline so you can cover the court as best you can. (**Note:** where you stand at the net depends on your opponent's position.) Be aware that the left hand's hold on the racquet produces grip changes. Your left hand pulls the racquet back as you turn left and then releases it for the backhand volley. For a forehand volley, push your racquet toward your right with the left hand as you turn your upper body to the right, and you'll be ready for a firm forehand shot. •

THE SHOELACE VOLLEY

For a low volley, use your downward and forward motion in meeting the ball to build momentum for the hit. With a firm grip, open the racquet face to send the ball over the net, stopping arm motion on contact. The result is a shot with good speed and accuracy that will clear the net. It will also have some backspin that will keep it low after it bounces in your opponent's court.

You can use this low volley with spectacular results from anywhere in the court, even when caught behind the service line or somewhere in the backcourt. The ball may be at your feet before the bounce, and you can still make a good return shot.

1. Stand behind the service line. Have a friend feed you 20 to 30 balls from the other side of the net. They should reach you at knee level or below. Keep returning them until you have the shoelace volley down.
2. Stand at the baseline. Have your friend feed you 4 to 5 low balls that force you to come forward to hit them on the fly. Each toss should make you come a little closer to the net. Return to the baseline and repeat several times. Then have your friend alternate balls to your forehand and backhand as you come forward. When you reach the net, return to the baseline and start over. ●

the lob and smash

9

The Lob

The *lob* is a ball hit above the reach of a player near the net. With the type of topspin strokes you've been learning, you just need to lift the ball higher to produce a good lob. Open the racquet face, still hitting with topspin, and lift the ball 15 to 20 feet over the net.

Although the ball may be slower than a hard ground stroke, this shot still needs plenty of racquet speed and a lot of topspin to make the ball bounce past your opponent's service line. The topspin helps bring the ball down sooner and faster, making it jump toward the back fence so that your opponent will find it difficult if not impossible to reach the ball and return it. This topspin shot used to be very unusual two decades ago, but today it's common among the top pros.

Another way of achieving a lob—especially useful when you're having a difficult time reaching the ball—is simply to open the racquet face under the ball and hit it up. It will probably be a slow ball, but if you hit it 25 feet or more in the air and deep into your opponent's court, it will give you time to return to a more comfortable position in your court. This topspin shot is usually called a *defensive lob*. The deeper you hit a defensive lob into your opponent's court, the more difficulty he or she will have smashing it back.

The Smash

When your opponent tries to lob the ball over your head, you *smash* it back, meaning you hit an overhead shot when it is right above you. A smash requires only short preparation and is between a high volley and a serve. The most important thing in the smash is to find the ball well with your racquet. The easiest place to do that is above your head, slightly in front of you. Move under the ball as if you want it to land on your head or as if you were going to catch it. Extend your nonhitting arm upward.

The best smashers lift the racquet with both hands, coordinating this move with the upward

Follow the soaring ball with both hands (right).

flight of the ball. Then, as the ball begins descending, they point to it with the left hand, as if catching it. Then they hit the ball. If the lob is clearly moving behind their immediate reach, they do not move backward while still facing the net. Instead they turn to run back while still raising the racquet slowly and looking at the ball over the left arm. When the ball is within their reach, they jump with a scissor-like leg action, which allows a timely power release and avoids twisting the lower back or falling. (See Play Like the Pros: Grabbing the Smash, page 178.)

Smashes don't need much force to be fast and effective. They require coordination and timing, with the force applied when the racquet is almost touching the ball.

Smashes usually come out harder than intended, especially in the early learning stages. For your playing partner's safety, smash gently and with control.

Note: When you don't have a friend who can hit or throw high balls to you, feel free to toss them high yourself and do the drills below. Toss each ball high enough so it clears your head after the bounce. Find the ball well as it starts to come down for the second time and hit into the opposing court. Advanced players sometimes practice this way, hitting the ball up with the racquet, letting it bounce up once, and then smashing it down into the other court. Remember, you want to practice control rather than force while doing these drills. The force is within you—the control has to be learned.

- Stand close to the net without your racquet. Have a friend, positioned on the other side of the net and to your right side, toss balls to you a little higher than your head. Hit them down into the opponent's court with your right hand, without hitting your friend (see top left photo next page).
- Have your friend stand on the other side of the net safely to one side. Hold your racquet by the throat with the right hand. Have your friend toss balls above your head. Hit them down into the opponent's court (see top right photo next page). Do this gently, with control.
- Move your hand gradually down the racquet grip. Hit several smashes at each hand position, mastering the new racquet length before going on to the next. When reaching up for the ball, lift your racquet with the help of your left hand. Maneuver yourself under the ball, using your left

Push the ball over the net with a downward motion (left).

With your racquet short, push the ball down but over the net (right).

With the left hand, lift the racquet above your head (left).

Follow the ball with both hands, positioning yourself underneath (right).

*Find the ball slowly with
your racquet and only then
accelerate (left).*

*Finish by your left hip,
catching the racquet with
your left hand (right).*

hand to point to the ball as if you were catching it. Your racquet drops a
bit behind your back, but not as much as in a serve. When the ball drops
within your reach, release your right arm power into the shot and connect with the ball. Follow through firmly rather than forcefully. Continue
the arm motion in the direction of your left hip to prevent hitting your legs
with the racquet. End with the throat of the racquet in your left hand,
poised to return the racquet to the volleying ready position. See photos
bottom of opposite page and this page. ●

GRABBING THE SMASH

Although it's a good and common practice to point to the ball as you move to position yourself under a high lob for a thunderous overhead smash, I recommend a more complete action that produces better results. While pointing to the ball, follow it as if trying to grab it with your left hand. Maneuver your body until you can strike it with ease. Pancho Gonzales, who had perhaps the greatest overhead smash of all time, once told me, "Don't try to hit the smash. Just find the ball well and then release the stroke." It's best to start raising your racquet with the left hand still on the throat, then release the left hand to point to the ball. Unlike a fully developed serve with the long, looping motion of the racquet before the hit, lift your racquet straight up, as in the high forehand volley.

One of the greatest drills to clarify how to hit the smash is to crowd the net while a friend feeds you short lobs. Hit the ball down hard so that it tends to bounce over the back fence. The end result is a downward stroke that is useful in any situation, including a difficult lob that has driven you back from the net behind the service line. The only difference between a challenging smash from the backcourt and one you hit near the net is the racquet angle. When farther back on the court, open the racquet face more to make the ball clear the net while still hitting the smash down, regardless of the distance. This drill clarifies further that serves are hit up and the smash down.

On difficult smashes, use a **scissor kick** to help balance yourself while you strike. While you lean backward to reach for the ball, you raise the left leg forward for balance. When you jump to strike, the right leg shoots forward while the left leg snaps back in a scissor motion. Time it wisely and naturally so you don't fall. •

scoring

10

Gustavo Kuerten. [Art Seitz]

TENNIS SCORING is made up of a series of games. Each game is made up of four or more points. One player serves for one game, and the other player serves for the next game, alternating back and forth. The player who is returning the serve can only hit the ball after it has bounced in the service court. Once the ball is served, it is in play until one of the players hits the ball into the net, hits the ball outside his opponent's court, or is unable to hit the ball before it bounces twice. The player who did not make the mistake earns one point, and the server puts the ball in play again to start the next point.

The Origin of Scoring

The way points are counted in tennis may seem peculiar. The system was adopted in the nineteenth century and has remained almost unchanged since then. With the advent of televised tennis matches, officials added tiebreakers to prevent marathon matches—see pages 184–85. The scoring system was born during a tennis match held on a court with a broken clock beside it, which the players used to keep score: One player used the hour hand of the clock; the other the minute hand. When the player using the minute hand won a point, he moved his hand ahead a quarter of an hour, to the fifteen-minute mark. Thus the first point resulted in a score of 15–love (*love* meaning *zero*). When he won another point, he moved the minute hand another fifteen minutes, to the half-hour position (the score was now 30–love). If the other player won the next point, he moved the hour hand of the clock to the fifteen-minute mark (the score was now 30–15). If the first player won the next point, he moved his minute hand to the forty-minute mark (the score was now 40–15).

There was one requirement, however; he had to win the game by a minimum of two points. If the other player had also advanced his hand

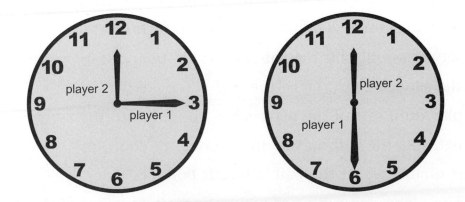

15-love (left).

30-love (right).

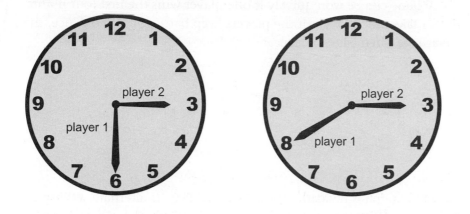

30-15 (left).

40-15 (right).

to the forty-minute mark, the score, being even, was called *deuce* (from *deus*, the Old French word for *two*). This meant that there were still two points to be made (and only twenty minutes left on the clock face). So the next point won allowed that player to advance his hand to the forty-five-minute mark, a score called *advantage* because that player now had the advantage for winning the game. If the player with the advantage won the next point, he would win the game. If the other player won the next point, they would both be back at deuce. Instead of the player who had just won the point moving his hand forward to the forty-five-minute mark, the one who had just lost his point would move his hand back to the forty-minute mark.

The keeping of score was customized later by having only the server announce the score (rather than either of the players), calling his score first followed by the opponent's score.

Deuce (left).

Advantage (right).

A game can be won quickly if one player wins the first four points, or can take much longer if the players keep battling back to deuce, then advantage, then back to deuce.

Game, Set, Match

A tennis match is divided into several *sets*. Players alternate serving one game each until one of them wins six games. This player now has won one set. Just as each game must be won by a margin of two points, each set must be won by a margin of two games. The score can be 6–0, 6–1, 6–2, 6–3, or 6–4 for someone to win a set. If the score reaches 5–5, play continues until one player wins 7–5 (seven games won to five lost).

If the score reaches 6–6 (6-all), then a tiebreaker game is played. The player who wins the tiebreaker game wins the set 7–6.

In most tournament matches, three sets are played. In major championships, men play five sets; women play three. A few major tournaments don't play tiebreakers in the final set. Instead, a player must win by two games (8–6, 12–10, or 16–14, for example).

Winning a match that requires three sets means winning two sets. The result can be 2 sets to 0, or 2 sets to 1, if each player wins one of the first two sets. The third and deciding set is called the *final set*. A three-match set usually lasts between one hour and two-and-a-half hours. In five-set matches, a player must win three sets. Some of these matches can last four to five hours; the record is over six hours.

To start a match, a player spins a tennis racquet or tosses a coin to decide who will serve first and from which end of the court. To spin the racquet, the player holds the butt between his fingers and stands the head on the ground. When he spins the butt like a top, the other player says "Up" or "Down." When the racquet falls, the manufacturer's logo, printed on the butt, will be either face up or down. The winner of the toss or spin can either choose to serve first or choose which end of the court to take for the first game. If the winner decides to serve or return, his opponent can choose which end to play. If the winner chooses the end, his opponent chooses whether to serve or return the serve.

You might think choosing to serve first would be the best strategy, but which end you play from can also be important. Most courts are built facing approximately north–south, so the angle of the sun varies according to the time of the day, affecting players more on one end than the other. This is usually an issue when you toss the ball for a serve. Players usually choose the end where the sun is behind them for the first game in which they serve. Remember that a left-hander faces at a different angle to the sun when serving than a right-hander. A left-hander playing a right-hander (or a right-hander playing a left-hander) may defer the first choice to his opponent. For example, if his opponent chooses to serve, the left-hander should choose to have his opponent serve from the side that most causes him to look into the sun when serving. Next, when he serves the following game, he is on his "good" side.

Players change the end of the court they are playing on after each odd-numbered sum of games (one game, three games, five games, etc.) in each set. After each set, if the sum of games is an odd number, players change ends. If the set reaches a tiebreaker, players start the new set at the opposite end from where they started the previous set.

THE SERVING ADVANTAGE

Usually, a good server is in command in the early stages of a point. The player has the advantage of a serve that may be difficult to return with precision, so the player returning a serve opts for a safe return. This gives the server an easier ball to handle, which can be used to pressure the opponent by hitting a tough ball to return. A great return of serve changes that advantage, but statistically, in professional tennis, the serving player ends up winning the serve more times than not. When one player loses a game he was serving, it is called a *service break*.

SAMPLE SCORING SEQUENCE

Let's say you won the toss and have decided to serve, letting your opponent choose the starting end of the court. Go to the other end, behind the baseline, with one ball in your left hand and one in your pocket. Always start a game by serving from the right side of the court.

Serve the first point crosscourt to your opponent's service court. If you miss the first serve, you serve a second one. If you miss again, it's a double fault and the point goes to your opponent. Whoever wins the first point has the score of 15. Because the server's points are called first, the score is now either 15–love if you won the point or love–15 if you lost the point.

Now you serve from the left side. If the score is 15–love, and you win this point, the score is now 30–love. If your opponent won this point, the score is 15–15 (15-all). If you lost the first two points, the score is love–30.

Continue alternating sides of your court, serving one point from the right and one from the left. Let's say you go from 15-all to 30–15 to 30-all. If you win the next point, the score is 40–30. If you win the next point, you win the game. Then as far as the set is concerned, you are at 1–love. You, the server, have won one game; your opponent has won none.

You then change sides of the court, and your opponent serves the next game. If you reach 40–40 (40-all, or deuce), whoever wins the next point is at advantage—either *advantage to the server (ad-in)*, or *advantage to the receiver (ad-out)*. If the player at advantage wins the next point, he wins the game. If not, the score goes back to deuce. There is no limit to the number of deuces that can occur in a game. As an exception, some school competitions use a no-ad scoring system, whereby the player winning the first point after 40 wins the game.

Each player serves one game, and then the other player serves the next game, until one player wins the set by winning six games before his opponent. As covered earlier, if the score reaches 6–6, a tiebreaker is played and the set ends 7–6.

TIEBREAKERS

A tiebreaker is scored and played a bit differently from regular games. The player whose turn it is to do so serves the first point from the right side of the court. After the first point, his opponent serves the next two points, the first from the left side and the next one from the right. After that, the serve goes back to the first player, who serves two points, the first from the left side, the next one from the right. As in a regular game, the rule of calling out the server's points first is used during the tiebreaker. At a tournament, on the other hand, umpires calling the score usually preface the score with the leading player's name: "Ms. Johnson, 4 points to 3."

The serve keeps switching back and forth between players; each player serves two points and alternates between the right and left sides of the court. Tiebreaker points are counted 1, 2, 3, and so on. The first player to reach seven points wins the tiebreaker—as long as he or she has achieved a margin of at least two points. If players are closely matched, a tiebreaker can go on for a long time, until one player wins by at least two points, to scores like 12–10. Whoever wins the tiebreaker wins that set.

Once the tiebreaker is over, the players move to the opposite end from which they started the previous set. In the first game of the next set, the player who received the first serve in the previous set starts serving. The score of a set that was won with a tiebreaker is written 7–6, with the points scored by the loser of the tiebreaker in parentheses: 7–6 (8). A sample score for a three-set match might look like this: 7–6 (3), 6–7 (8), 6–3. Ms. Johnson won the first set in a tiebreaker (7–3 points), lost the second set in another tiebreaker (10–8 points), and won the third set (6-3 games). Usual changeover rest periods are 90 seconds when changing sides during a set and 120 seconds between sets.

11 playing the singles game

Roger Federer. [Art Seitz]

Singles Strategies

The best game philosophy is to keep the ball in play, even when playing a standard match at club level. Don't hit toward your opponent but slightly away from him to make him work at it, then hit to the open court when you have a sure shot. If you keep the ball in play without making silly errors, you'll slowly learn to win points. It may surprise you how many people—perhaps 90 percent of the 50 million or so who play tennis around the world—cannot hit twenty balls firmly back and forth in the court.

In club play, more points are lost on mistakes or unforced errors than are won by hitting winners. If you keep the ball in play, you'll end up winning more points than you'll lose. Rallying is the part to learn first.

In a match on any medium-to-slow court, professionals rally before trying to hit winners. You should do the same. Hit your ball 3 to 4 feet over the net with power and plenty of topspin, not only to be safe, but also for depth and higher bounce. This will force your opponent to return from farther back, reducing his chances of hitting a winner or an angled placement that can catch you unprepared.

MARGIN FOR ERROR

If your opponent has a weak backhand, or his forehand is a much bigger weapon than his backhand, direct your shots to his backhand side. If your opponent's game is balanced, hit most of your shots crosscourt or down the middle, over the lower part of the net. Avoid making errors or opening up your court. When you start sensing where your opponent is vulnerable, hit the ball there, always keeping a good margin for error. For example, if you know that in practice you need to aim 3 feet inside the sideline to avoid hitting out in a down-the-line shot, do the same in a match. The same goes for height over the net: if aiming 1 foot over the net results in too many hits into the net during practice, then during a match hit the ball at least 2 feet over the net, using plenty of topspin.

DEPTH

If the ball is bouncing too short in your opponent's court, hit it higher. You'll achieve more depth and more jump on your shot. It is far less dangerous to hit the ball closer to the service line than to go for the baseline. And it doesn't make sense to hit the ball long when you have enough topspin to make it land well inside the court and make it jump.

ATTACKING SHORT BALLS

After you hit a forceful shot, move a few steps into your court. Your opponent will likely respond with a shorter or easier shot. As you move forward for a shorter ball, hit your ground strokes lower and with more topspin by closing the racquet face and pulling up more on the stroke, making sure to clear the net. An upward effort and more topspin are needed because the ball has a shorter trajectory to be lifted over the net and then go down into your opponent's court. The same goes for passing shots. They need to be hit with plenty of topspin so the ball will dip down soon after crossing the net, making it more difficult for your opponent to volley.

DRIFTING BACK TO THE CENTER

When you hit a good crosscourt shot from the backcourt and your opponent is also back, drift slowly toward the middle. It is very likely that your opponent will hit crosscourt, the best percentage shot for him. Don't run toward the center of the court, or you will create an opening for your opponent to hit to the place you just left. If your opponent shoots down the line, close to the sideline, as you drift to the center, he'll be risking much more. But you'll be facing slightly in that direction as you drift toward the middle, so you'll just need to pivot and accelerate to reach the ball. If your opponent hits behind you, pivot back and you should be close to the path of the ball.

HITTING CROSSCOURT

When you are pulled wide, which occurs mostly when receiving a crosscourt shot, hit the ball back crosscourt, so that you don't open the court much to your opponent. A weak shot, of course, is a setup for him. It will be short and allow him to attack you on either side, to come to the net, etc. But if you hit the ball hard and with plenty of topspin, he won't be able to do something surprising with it.

If you don't have a strong crosscourt shot but are pulled wide, lift the ball high, down the middle, and past your opponent's service line. This tactic will give you plenty of time to return to the middle of your court, ready for his next shot.

At a high level of play, a crosscourt shot takes precedence over any other shot as a return of a good crosscourt shot. The exception would be your opponent has stayed too close to the side he made the shot from, leaving the other side wide open for your down-the-line shot. Top pros engage in crosscourt rallies mixed with down-the-middle shots, risking nothing, waiting for a weaker shot that opens the play for something different.

To show you how dangerous down-the-line shots can be when you are pulled wide, imagine yourself playing someone good. You hit only down the line, while the other player hits only good crosscourt shots. In a short time, you are out of breath because you are running many more yards to get to each shot than your opponent. A good crosscourt shot pulls you beyond your sideline so that your down-the-line shot can't be parallel to the sideline, or else it lands outside your opponent's court. You have to angle your shot toward his court. After the bounce, the ball will continue to approach the middle, giving him a good chance to cross it the other way, where you left a wide-open court. This forces you to race all the way across your court. A few shots like that, and you feel like you are chasing a rabbit, while your opponent strolls around the court. You may also start to hit short, allowing your opponent to come to the net.

STUDYING YOUR OPPONENT

You need to adjust your game tactics to your opponent's play. Stay cool and see what gives him trouble, what he likes, and what throws him off. Unless you know your opponent well, "feel" him or her at the beginning of a match. Mix in some junk shots with your good shots. Many players don't handle a change of pace well. Others thrive on your hard shots, making you feel that the better you are playing, the better they play. Throw some high topspin shots that bounce deep and high and see how your opponent reacts. If he has trouble, keep it up. It's part of the game. If you are playing competitively, you are not there to hand the match to your opponent, but to beat him, or at least to have him sweat it out until the last point is over.

PRACTICE MATCHES

Practice matches or social matches are different. You try to get the best workout possible. Sometimes your friend across the net doesn't have a good backhand. If you hit mostly to your friend's forehand, you'll get the best possible practice, only reverting to winning tactics if you need to. When practicing, focus on consistency and accuracy, rather than raw power. You can hit hard but use a lot of topspin. The tendency in tournament matches is to hit forward, flattening out the stroke. Practice the other way around. Accustom your muscles to lifting the ball. It will be easier to resort to topspin in tight spots in tournament play.

RUSHING THE NET

When you approach the net, whether with your forehand or backhand, a down-the-line approach will cut the angle of your opponent's passing shot. In other words, after you hit the ball, continue to advance, keeping to the side from which you made the approach—perhaps 2 to 3 feet from the centerline depending on your shot's depth and how close you advance to the net. Your opponent will have only a small opening to pass you with a sharp and short crosscourt. See illustration below.

For the average player such a sharp angle is a low percentage shot. Unless he has plenty of topspin, he'll have to resort to hitting a slow shot to place the ball in the open space, giving you a chance to run it down.

DEFENDING AGAINST A NET RUSHER

If you are in your backcourt, and your opponent has made a good approach that doesn't give you much angle to pass him, you can *dink* the ball—hit it so low and slow or with so much topspin that the ball goes down to his feet or to his side. From there, your opponent will have trouble volleying with pace, which will usually give you a shorter ball and a better chance to pass him with your next shot. If your opponent is very close to the net, your best choice is a good lob, making sure you send the ball well over him even if he jumps back and up. As a dink usually drives your opponent close to the net, the lob is a good follow-up shot.

BACKCOURT TACTICS

Let's say you are a right-hander playing a right-hander. A very good tactic for you is to stay in the backcourt, a little to the left of the center.

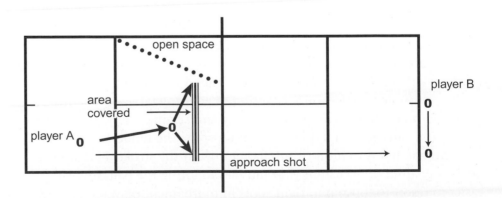

Net player's coverage.

Pound the ball into your opponent's backhand, again and again, using a backhand crosscourt and forehand inside out—where a forehand is angled to the right, as opposed to the more normal crosscourt shot to the left.

Whenever possible, run around your backhand (i.e., run beyond the ball's path to hit a forehand instead of a backhand), hitting inside-out forehands across to the right. Your opponent will keep trying to force you to hit the weaker backhand shots, and to do so, he will have to send the ball closer to your left sideline and possibly out of play. After every strong shot, especially with your forehand, move a yard inside your court, staying still slightly to the left of the center, ready for a weaker return. After a while, your opponent will feel pressured. There's not much room for a crosscourt backhand, and he'll risk sending the ball down the line. If he makes a good shot, run it down and hit it with plenty of topspin, high and safely, toward the middle of his backhand side. Then move into the court again, toward the left, and keep pounding his backhand side. As soon as he makes a weaker shot, jump on it crosscourt with your forehand, sharply angled and with plenty of topspin. It should be a safe shot if you produce enough topspin, and your opponent will have a hard time reaching it and even more difficulty handling it. If by then you are at the net, you probably have a big open court for your volley and an easy put-away or smash.

This strategy requires a lot of patience and very good stamina. Some pros with a big forehand sometimes park themselves 2 to 3 feet to the left of the center of the court, pounding their forehands patiently to their opponent's backhand side or hitting sharp crosscourt shots when the ball comes to their backhand. They wait for the short ball they can attack savagely, hitting far from their opponent's reach. When they reach the net, the point is almost won. Unless their opponent, risking everything, hits a miraculous winner or an incredible angle shot, fate is in the hands of the attacking player.

FIRST-SERVE PERCENTAGE

Hitting your first serve in is a very good way to put more pressure on your opponent. Even a slower first serve is treated with more respect than a second serve of the same speed. If you miss your first serve consistently, the other player will soon be attacking your second serve and making better returns. You can do the same if your opponent misses his first serve. Move inside the court and attack his second serve.

CROSSCOURT SERVICE RETURNS

The safest return of serve is usually crosscourt, over the lowest part of the net and toward the longest extension of the court. When an opponent is coming to the net following his serve, pounding the ball crosscourt will give good results: the ball will dip down sooner than a down-the-line shot, and its speed will make it difficult for your opponent to

SWITCHING AMONG COURT SURFACES

Many players have had the opportunity to play on more than one surface, such as Har-Tru or Fast Dry courts (green clay), red clay, hard courts, or carpet. Changing from one type of surface to another requires making adjustments both on timing the ball and in your swing. Hard courts can also vary in speed according to their composition. Adding more fine sand to the paint mix, for example, makes the surface slower because it creates more friction on the bounce. There are differences even among the same type of clay courts, depending on how damp the court is. Grass courts play faster when they are damp. Indoor carpets at different clubs can differ in texture, too. Some players have difficulty adjusting to different court surfaces. Your main focus should be on stalking the ball after the bounce, so you can adjust your timing to the flight. As satisfying as it is to hit the ball hard and fast, it is far better to lose some ball speed in the first few minutes of your adjustment than miss and lose confidence. Of course, you'll have more time on clay, especially red clay. The tendency, therefore, when changing from clay to hard courts is to rush. But, as you know, if you rush on any surface you'll be in trouble, especially on hard courts. Take your racquet back early, and you'll be caught with your racquet behind, or you'll have to force it forward too fast, losing control.

To counteract the tendency to rush, shorten your preparation on hard courts. Keep the racquet in front longer, closer to the ball than usual, and then swing. Make sure you accelerate with the ball already on your strings. Rather than following the ball with your racquet, swing up and across the body to brush it more and increase control.

Overall, let your body tell you how it wants to move on the surface you are playing. Forcing your footwork unnaturally is a primary cause of leg, hip, and lower back injuries in tennis.

Be a natural. In this sense, copy the pros. ●

THE ZONE—CALMNESS AND TRANQUILLITY

How do top pros achieve such a state of confidence and achievement? Where a normal human being would succumb under the pressure, top pros usually look serene. Eight thousand people in the stands cheering or cursing them, and they're still able to perform. Not only in tennis, but in other sports as well, many top performers exemplify a state of calm tranquillity that may seem difficult to achieve.

Let's define nervousness. It is usually the feeling resulting from considering too many things or possibilities within a short period of time. Would you be nervous if you knew your exact course of action? Probably not.

Another cause of nervousness is looking around too much, causing you to receive too many pieces of information. This again impedes focusing on one thing: your contact with the ball.

To solve nervousness or lack of focus, some of the top tennis players perform exercises prior to a match. Billie Jean King, for instance, would sit at a table staring at a ball for a good period of time until she no longer felt compelled to look somewhere else.

A useful habit between points is to look at something far away, keeping your eyes there at least for a few seconds. You'll feel calmer, more space, and more in control of things around you.

Overall, think as little as possible, and stay in present time. Don't rush. Keep your attention on the ball, try to see its seams, and focus—first on feeling the contact point and then on the full finish of the stroke. Always be aware of the feel of the ball on the strings, ideally as a brushing action, no matter how short, rather than a straight hit. Focusing on this calms your mind. Also, if you feel the contact, you're more likely to remember that particular feel during the game and be able to repeat it consistently.   •

return. It may even pass him by. This tactic reduces your risk compared with hitting a down-the-line return of serve, closer to the sideline and over the higher part of the net.

STEADY TACTICS

Of course, you would vary all these tactics depending on the degree of success your opponent has in handling them. You can surprise your opponent with a change here and there, but keep winning tactics steady. Don't change a winning game—but always change a losing one. Don't vary winning tactics just for the sake of change. It might give your opponent a lift and change the whole match.

The same goes for your basic game. You know your best weapons. If you have the fundamentals of this book down well, your consistency will be very high. Stick to your topspin and the finish of your ground strokes. They will keep the ball in the court, and you won't have to resort to hybrid strokes.

Stay in the match as long as possible. Don't rush. Keep the ball in play one time more than your opponent, and you'll beat players that look much flashier than you.

Overall, respect your opponents and their shots. Never underestimate anyone. If you can beat some opponents easily, do so without snubbing them. They will appreciate your game and your behavior. They will also know that the points or games they won were won on their own, and you didn't hand them anything they didn't earn.

And if one player keeps beating you no matter how well you play or how hard you try, recognize that he or she is better than you are at this point in time. Keep playing your best and learn from the experience. It is possible to improve every day, to learn something good every day. And we learn something every day, whether we recognize it or not. A positive experience depends only on *you*.

playing
the doubles game

Roger Federer. [Art Seitz]

Doubles
Strategies

A tennis doubles game can be a work of art. While singles tends to be a game of power, stamina, speed, and strong will, doubles is a game of touch, placement, cleverness, and above all, teamwork.

First of all, I hope you enjoy your partner, either as a person or as a player—ideally both. In doubles play, the variables and changing momentum of a game can be so great that you need a partner whose emotional style complements your (hopefully) calm and measured responses.

As you play, try to remain analytical rather than becoming judgmental of your partner's game. Concentrating on resolving the technical and tactical aspects of the game tends to keep your reactions (and your partner's) under control. Otherwise, if either of you becomes wrapped up in heated emotions, discomfort is likely to arise and dissipate the pleasure of this wonderful game. So overall, be a master of your own behavior and show true professionalism and sportsmanship no matter how much of an advanced player or a beginner you may be, or how you happen to be playing on any given day.

If you're still a newcomer to the game, at least to the game of doubles, you'd do well to choose a partner who is an accomplished player, appreciates your interest and progress, and is willing to be your personal guru for this specific match. Or choose a friend who is a newcomer too, but who welcomes a good laugh and has the ability to turn new situations and challenging experiences into fun.

THE SERVE

Simplicity of choice applies to the serve in doubles. It is most effective to spin your first serve into your opponent's weaker shot, usually the backhand, with a high-kicking spin. This lets you take command of the point right there, rather than risking a hard first serve, missing it, and thus empowering your opponent to ram the return. Statistics show that the single most important factor in winning a professional doubles match is the percentage of first serves successfully hit into the court.

Beware of serving wide near the singles line, allowing your opponent to hit a searing down-the-line return. If you intend to serve wide, advise your partner so he or she will be prepared to cover the down-the-line shot if needed.

When in doubt, serve to the centerline. You'll open less of your court for the opposition to hit into. Be patient, serving to your opponent's weakness, such as a weak backhand that can be poached by your partner. Notice where your opponents miss the most, and aim there.

PLACING THE BALL

In doubles, it is far more effective to place the ball where your opponents have difficulty handling it, rather than blasting it as hard as you can. And where does your shot hurt them the most? At their feet and away from the partner at the net.

Assuming you and your partner have mastered the fundamentals of the volley, the basic doubles strategy puts alternating players up near the net and back near the baseline, either serving or returning a serve. During the game your partner is serving, you stay near the net practically all the time.

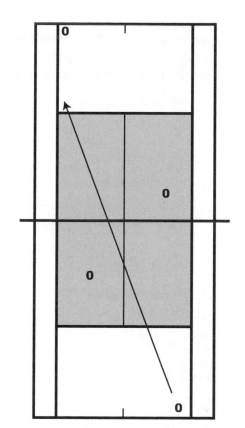

Each team puts a player at net. The player returning the serve tries to hit crosscourt to keep the ball away from the net player.

Typically, your opponents put a player at the net before the point starts, while the other obviously stays back to return your serve. Your team's goal, first of all, is to keep any shot away from the net player. This is also your opponents' goal, so the return of your serve is likely to come back to you crosscourt. In general, crosscourt shots are the easiest and safest solutions, and especially effective when hit low, because they are harder to attack or to volley back. Statistics show that the team who makes the fewest mistakes and keeps the ball traveling mainly crosscourt is more likely to win than a team who constantly mixes shots.

Lobs are also a good tactic, but lob high and deep to avoid exposing your partner to a hard overhead smash, dangerous both tactically and physically. The same risk exists with high returns, which the opposing net player can reach and then volley forcefully straight into your partner.

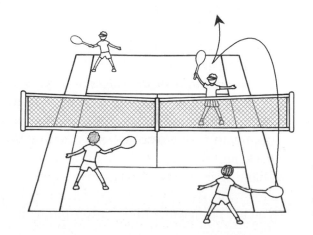

Lob high and deep to make the net player go back for the ball or make the backcourt player cross the whole court to reach it.

If you are the player in the backcourt, keep the ball crosscourt and low. Topspin is a good way to place the ball low in the court, preferably delivered to the feet of an advancing opponent. Or, if your opponent stays back, topspin lets you power the ball hard, deep, and crosscourt, keeping the ball in play and avoiding unforced errors.

Ouch! Avoid a short lob or easy-to-reach return that gives your opposing net player a chance to wallop your partner.

This is where having an aggressive and attentive partner pays off. The net player patiently waits at his or her half of the net for the first opportunity to cut off an opponent's shot and volley it back to win the point. Patience is key. In some points, the net player doesn't have this opportunity and never hits the ball. If you're at the net, your best choice is to place the volley down the center of the court. You'll make fewer errors down the middle, aiming between your opponents, than by going for either sideline. The same goes for the overhead smash. Even top pros make the down-the-middle choice in tough situations, minimizing their risk of an unforced error.

If you're serving, and are fast and confident in your volleys, you can follow your serve (and any service returns) by moving forward to the net. On the way there, you may have to hit your first volley around the service line. Again, your first choice is to volley crosscourt, firmly but safely, and then keep closing in on the net but now moving at a slower pace. You don't want to get too close to the net and risk a good lob passing overhead, out of your reach.

At least in the early stages of playing doubles, the primary team strategy is for one player to stay back and the other to be near the net, making the game a bit like "cat and mouse." You tease your backcourt opponent with crosscourt shots, hitting harder if he or she is staying back, and softer, with more topspin, down at the feet if the player is charging forward. This sets up your net partner for the kill. Keep hitting crosscourt without coming dangerously close to the doubles sidelines. If you are proficient with your topspin, you can tease your opponent with harder topspin shots, landing deeper behind the service line, and then hit some shorter balls crosscourt while your partner stalks the net, stealthily poised to make the decisive, winning move.

Some opponents at the net have a tendency to *poach* by reaching into the backcourt partner's territory to cut off shots with a surprise volley. If this happens, make it look like you are going to hit crosscourt, wait a moment until the net player commits to leaning in toward the centerline, and then hit the ball behind him, down the line.

Sometimes a medium-height, down-the-line topspin shot (about 8 feet above the net) is harder to reach than a regular drive just above the net.

You can cloak your shots by waiting slightly longer than usual before hitting, thereby teasing your

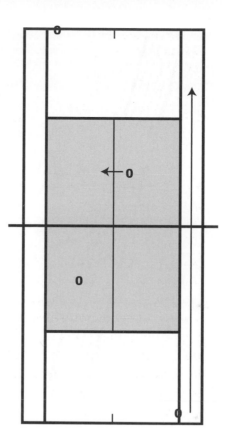

If your opponent at net commits toward the center, hit behind and down the line.

net-hugging opponent into second-guessing what you will do. In this microsecond wait, the net player tends to drop off the balls of his feet and, standing flat-footed, he will not be able to react to a keen down-the-line passing shot.

THE TUNNEL CONCEPT

Overall, the basic doubles tactic for the player in the backcourt is to view the court as a narrow crosscourt tunnel, down which to send the balls. Pros are keenly aware of the importance of this crosscourt tunnel concept and sometimes practice it intensely with just two players on the court.

You need to stay aware of more than the ball in the doubles game. If at some point the opposing net player does something devilish, like stepping into the tunnel to cut off your crosscourt shot, just set aside the tunnel state of mind. The whole court now becomes fair game. Mindful

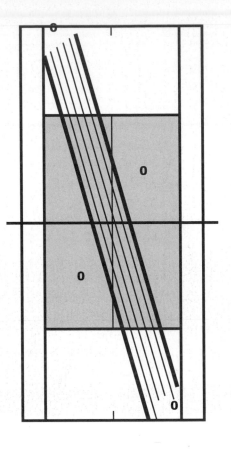

Work on seeing the doubles court as a tunnel, with the backcourt players hitting deep crosscourt shots away from the net players.

of your opponents' tactics, which could easily mirror your own, you'll learn to have some mischievous ideas of ways to disrupt their game.

THE PARTNER CONNECTION

You and your partner should play as if connected by an invisible cord. If you are on the backcourt and move to the right to reach a shot, your partner at the net should move toward the center just as far as you moved to the side to cover the court you left open. The longer you play together, the more instinctive and natural this attention to your partner's moves becomes.

In professional tennis, this coordinated teamwork extends to both players; they move forward aggressively or backward defensively in unison, depending on the effectiveness of their shots. If you watch a pro match, you'll sometimes see both players charging the net together, hoping to intimidate their opponents.

Doubles play can be tremendous fun, especially with good communication between partners. Be inventive within these strategies and nurture your partner, and you will both become masters of this beautiful game.

PERFORMING WELL IN A MATCH

Most players tend to rush their preparation and strokes in match play. In tournaments, when their timing is good, they do fine. But in many cases, a player who practices his game with ease and confidence becomes tight and nervous in a real match.

Most coaches (and players) blame this error on character, but character has little to do with it. Rushed timing is the underlying error, a technical flaw that can be resolved simply.

When players prepare early, they make mental images of what will happen to the ball instead of waiting and observing the ball's actual flight and speed. But consider the physics: on a hard court, a ball that started from one baseline at 50 mph usually arrives at the other baseline at about 20 mph. Imagine how much more it slows down on a clay court. Therefore if you're early, you cannot release your swing smoothly, and so you lose feel and confidence. The trick is to wait—just as you do in practice.

In doubles, partners can help each other stay calm by asking the other player to wait for the ball, whether or not they are rushing the net. Timing, as explained earlier, is the most important part of your game. ●

13 playing tennis with the wegner method

Justine Henin-Hardenne.
[Art Seitz]

A Game for Life

Tennis played in a natural, instinctive way is a beautiful and aesthetic sport, full of feel and athletic moves. It can develop both your body and your ability to focus. It's a game you can continue to enjoy well into your later years, improving your mastery all the time.

Learning to control the ball can be exciting for

beginners as they apply a few basics that make the game easy, as well as for experienced players who are always looking for ways to improve their feel and control—which are nearly synonymous in this sport.

The best tennis pros are artists who turn motion into an art form, with little or no thought involved, just like concert pianists at their best. They focus on the ball to such an extent that everything else is almost immaterial.

DEVELOPING THAT FEEL

When you're learning to play tennis, the less you have to remember, the easier it will be for you to develop a real feel for the game. That is how the top pros play, thinking as little as possible. They focus on the feel of the ball with simple, uncomplicated techniques that work for them.

Trust your instinct, your natural ability. The Wegner Method techniques let you use this natural instinct and put you on course to achieve your potential.

Your ability may be much higher than you or others ever thought possible. Surprise them and yourself. Set a goal for your game and advance toward it, applying what you have learned here. It's not as difficult as it may look. Simplicity is the key. Learn what to focus on and what to drop overboard, and you'll sail into new horizons and a better game.

STAYING COOL

Overall, be a master of control. Show it with your emotions and your behavior. Today's international championship rules penalize unsportsmanlike conduct, and smaller tournaments often enforce those rules at the local level. Sportsmanship is the best way to survive and to have fun playing the game.

Today's top players act like the supreme artists they are. Regardless of the media pressure for sensational stories or behavior, these pros respect the rules, each other, and the officials. They don't lose control or let emotions run rampant. Apply this rule of conduct at the club level as well.

Credit for keeping the game sportsmanlike is due to those who are regulating the sport. Tennis couldn't exist without the contributions from the many officials and volunteers who regulate, officiate, and promote the game. As tennis grows with the influx of new legions of

IMPROVING AND CORRECTING YOUR GAME

Tennis is a lifelong sport, and as you learn and play, you'll discover areas that you'll want to correct or improve upon. It is sometimes difficult to exchange or correct old habits for a new way of playing, but always the first step is to return to the basics. To correct a stroke and have these changes stick, you may need to exaggerate the new way, as described below.

If you generally rush to prepare, practice waiting with the racquet in front until well after the bounce, then taking a nice swing, exaggerate the finish of the stroke. Having to wait may make you feel as if you don't have enough time to swing, but try it, and you'll be surprised at the results.

If your problem is a big backswing, practice for a while with almost no backswing at all. Start your stroke below the ball, then exaggerate the end of the stroke.

If you turn sideways for your forehand, practice opening your stance so far that you place your right foot ahead of the left one (for a right-hander).

If you follow through straight on your forehand instead of brushing across your body, finish each forehand by tapping the racquet gently on your opposite shoulder (the left shoulder for right-handers) two or three times.

If you keep your arm straight through your ground strokes, start bending it right before the contact and continue bending it throughout the stroke.

If you hit down too soon on your serve, continue moving your arm and racquet upward after the impact, spinning the ball considerably.

If you hit your strokes too flat and too low, put a string 2 to 3 feet above the net. Practice hitting ground strokes over the string with plenty of topspin.

Review the drills in this book to help you analyze your strokes and determine what areas need work. The drills give you the precise techniques the top pros build their games on. These basics will become the foundation of your game. They simplify the learning process and will help you to keep improving day after day. Actually, tennis is an easy game to learn, once you know the basics laid out in this book. •

aficionados, media, tennis coaches, club managers, aspiring youngsters, and parents, the goal of staying cool is more critical than ever. Focus on the game and be a good sport no matter who wins a match, and you'll not only learn more and play better, but you'll also help keep tennis a dynamic, growing sport that you'll enjoy playing for a lifetime.

Troubleshooting

Here are some simple remedies for the most common problems you can face on a tennis court. The appropriate section of the book is referenced where applicable so you can easily find some tips and drills to help you.

DIFFICULTY	SOLUTION	SEE PAGE(S)
Ground Strokes		
Lacking ball control	Learn to find the ball first, then hit	39
Feeling rushed and lost	Take your time and notice how the ball slows down from baseline to baseline—close to 60 percent	61, 62
Thinking too much	Slow things down and focus on the ball exclusively	193
Hitting the ball into the net when you want to hit it hard	Aim the ball 2 to 3 feet over the net, with plenty of topspin, so you can still hit it hard and keep the ball in play	56–57, 204
Ground strokes land too short	Hit the ball higher over the net, or harder, or both	187
Hitting well, but ball seems to sail out	Hit the ball lower on the string bed, below the center, or close the racquet face, or both	45–46
Having trouble handling hard balls	Take a smaller backswing and use the incoming force across the racquet face	149–50
Rushing the shots	Count silently "1" at the bounce, then "2," "3," "4," and "5" when you hit	62
Not controlling the direction of the shot	Pay more attention to the racquet angle than to your body or your stroke	45–46
Hitting too wildly	Find the ball slowly, then accelerate your stroke	13, 112–13
Playing better against a hard hitter than a slow hitter	Wait longer for the ball and use more topspin, so you can hit hard without risking as much	53–55

DIFFICULTY	SOLUTION	SEE PAGE(S)
Hitting with topspin inconsistently	Position your racquet well under the ball at some point in your swing	91
Having difficulty timing and controlling the ball	Track the ball longer, especially after the bounce	61, 62

Forehand

DIFFICULTY	SOLUTION	SEE PAGE(S)
The ball comes out too flat	Use the windshield wiper motion, bending the arm, and lifting the elbow	91–95
Feeling the ball comes too close to the body	Use an open stance, keep your racquet in front longer, and hit in front	74, 80–82
The wrist breaks forward	Practice your windshield wiper forehand against a fence	93–95
No power	Combine an open stance with forceful bending of the arm	83–84
Wild power	Bring the arm closer to you in the follow-through, not farther away	18, 97
Forehand feels stiff	Loosen your wrist, lower your body, and then lift it as you hit	20
Racquet tends to turn	Hit the topspin forehand below the center of the string bed	53
Can't hit inside out	Lead the forehand with your hand, dragging the racquet behind it	69, 76

Two-Handed Backhand

DIFFICULTY	SOLUTION	SEE PAGE(S)
Stroke feels stiff	Let the left hand power the shot, with the right hand looser	103–4
Shot is too flat	Approach the ball from below, bend your arms, and finish over the shoulder	105–6
Hit too many backhands into the net	Aim 2 to 3 feet over the net, using topspin to make the ball drop	204
Ball sails out	Hit with more topspin to bring the ball down	112
No power	Use an open stance and bring your arms across the body	108
Racquet tends to turn	Keep racquet near the navel, separating the elbows; hit the ball below the center of the strings	153
Ball tends to go too far crosscourt	Drag the racquet head behind your hands, but still hit across your body	45–46

DIFFICULTY	SOLUTION	SEE PAGE(S)
Crosscourt shots go slightly out	Put more topspin on your crosscourt shots than on your down-the-line shots	56–57
Hitting the ball too short	Practice with a string placed 3 feet above the net, and hit over it	204

One-Handed Backhand

No power	Turn sideways, pointing the butt of the racquet to the ball; hit up and across to your right, squeezing your shoulder blades together and finishing high	123–24
No grip control on the topspin shot	Put your thumb behind the grip	114
Stroke feels stiff	Lift your body as you hit	123–24
Feeling too close to the ball	Hit the ball farther to your right and pull backward if needed to make more room for your shot	123–24
Hitting too many shots into the net	Swing up, ending with your arm extended and your hand well above the shoulder	123–24
Not meeting the ball in the right place	Track the ball with the butt of the racquet	115
Having trouble directing the ball	Extend both arms, with the hitting arm going up and toward the target and the other arm going backward and down	116
The racquet seems to collapse	Stay sideways and keep the racquet perpendicular to your arm	118–19
Having trouble finding the backhand grip	Change the grip as you turn to your left, pointing the butt of the racquet to the incoming ball	114–15

Backhand Slice

The ball has too much spin	Open the racquet initially, but flatten it as you hit	125–26
No power	Point to the ball with the butt of the racquet, then hit your slice not just forward but down and across to your right	127
Losing balance	Open both arms while hitting, and finish in a wide, inverted V	126
Having trouble timing the ball	Let the ball slide past your hand and into your racquet face before powering it	127

DIFFICULTY	SOLUTION	SEE PAGE(S)
Having trouble with the follow-through	Stay sideways and squeeze your shoulder blades closer together at the end of the swing	126
Slice approach floats	Hit down with a slightly open racquet	126–27
Slice keeps going into the net	Aim at least 1 foot over the net	124
Slice is too short	Aim 2 feet over the net and hold the finish	124
Slice is not consistent	Track the ball until it is near your hand; don't rush	127
The racquet is wobbly	Keep the throat of the racquet on your left hand until you are ready to hit, releasing it like a slingshot	126

The Serve

DIFFICULTY	SOLUTION	SEE PAGE(S)
Not finding the ball well	Imagine a small triangle between the tossing hand, the ball, and the racquet hand at the hit	134, 136
Toss is too low	Practice under a 12-foot ceiling until you can consistently toss the ball while barely touching the ceiling	
Toss is not consistent	Practice against a high wall or fence until the ball stays close to the wall or fence surface all the way	
No power	Go to a field and practice hitting a few balls as far as you can	144
No spin	Practice serving a bunch of balls over a fence, from 35 feet outside the court, giving them some spin	143
No pronation on the serve	Approach the ball with the racquet's edge in a hammerlike fashion, opening the racquet face when you hit	139
Hitting the legs at the end of the serve	Hit across the ball and to the right, turning the racquet before coming down in front toward the left hand	133–34
First serve is not consistent	Put some spin into the first serve, too	142–44
Coordination is off on the serve	Raise both arms together, and slow down or pause slightly before you hit	134, 136, 139
No control	Approach the ball slowly, then accelerate	134–36
Serve goes too long	Cock your wrist as if looking inside your palm	143–44

DIFFICULTY	SOLUTION	SEE PAGE(S)
Serve lands in the net too often	Serve up more; practice serving over a fence or a few feet over the net, with spin	143–44
Not enough spin	Let the racquet drop behind you and swing up and across to your right	139–40
Not enough power	Point at the ball with the butt of the racquet at some point before you hit it	142–44
Serve is too stiff	Bend your arm and then extend it	142–43
Body feels unbalanced while serving	Find a slightly sideways position before you start the serve and then turn into the ball as you hit	138
Serve feels too rushed	Start your serve slowly in the beginning, pause a bit, and then swing at the ball	136, 139
Toss is too erratic	Practice close to the court fence, tossing the ball and stopping it against the fence well above your head	
Double-faulting too often	Practice spinning the ball well above the net; you are only as good as your second serve	144–45

Return of Serve

DIFFICULTY	SOLUTION	SEE PAGE(S)
Mis-timing the return	Track the ball as long as possible after the bounce	147
Mis-timing a spin serve return	Keep your racquet in front as long as possible after the bounce	147
Mis-timing a hard serve return	Stop yourself from taking your racquet back too soon and too far	147, 149
Weak return of serve	The follow-through is the key to strong returns; to drive the ball, hit up and across instead of forward	151
Having a hard time returning a wide serve	Intercept the ball diagonally to cut off the angle and the distance to the ball	148
Having a hard time switching grips to return the serve	Wait with the weakest grip	145

Volleys

DIFFICULTY	SOLUTION	SEE PAGE(S)
Hitting too many forehand volleys into the net	Keep your elbow close to your stomach and lead the shot with the racquet's bottom edge	162

DIFFICULTY	SOLUTION	SEE PAGE(S)
Hitting too many backhand volleys into the net	Keep your elbow away from the body so as to open the racquet face	163–64, 165
Mis-hitting volleys	Wait until the ball is near before you punch	162
Feeling rushed	Count silently to 5, starting when your opponent hits the ball and hitting the volley on "5"	162
Having a hard time with low balls	Open the racquet face, and hit down and forward firmly	155–57, 172
Volley game not strong	Practice stopping the hand firmly right at or immediately after contact	155–57
Hitting high volleys out	Point the butt of the racquet toward the ball, then move the racquet butt down, closing the racquet face	166
Not controlling the placement	Pay more attention to the racquet angle, regardless of your body position	159
Feeling stiff at the net	Volley with your hands, not your body	158–59
Not knowing where to go at net	Follow the line of your shot, moving a bit to the right or left of the center as needed	190
Forgetting to split-step	It is not necessary to split-step; just let your body be ready to move forward or diagonally to intercept the next shot	169
Having trouble switching grips at net	Practice a hammer grip, with minimal changes as you take your racquet to either side	169–71
Racquet too wobbly	Keep your nonplaying hand on the throat of the racquet, pointing it up, and use the nonplaying hand to move your racquet to either side	169–71
Getting hit when at the net	React with your hands, not your body; use the racquet to protect yourself	162

Lobs

DIFFICULTY	SOLUTION	SEE PAGE(S)
Not knowing how high to aim a lob	The highest point of your aim should be past your opponent, not above him	173–74
Lobbing too short	Get under the ball more, and follow through with a full finish	173–74
Lobbing too long	Put more topspin in your lob	173–74

DIFFICULTY	SOLUTION	SEE PAGE(S)
Not controlling a defensive lob	Find the ball slowly before accelerating under it	173–74
Opponent reads the lob too well	Disguise the lob as a passing shot, changing it to a lob as late as possible	173–74
Not knowing where to go after hitting a lob	Make small moves to keep your opponent guessing which side you will cover most	
Not knowing whether to lob crosscourt or down the line	Lobbing over your opponent's backhand side is preferable, but crosscourt lobs are the safest of all	
Not knowing when to lob	If your opponent is crowding the net, a lob is due; if he is farther back, a topspin passing shot will draw him closer to the net, where you can pass him with a lob	190
Lobbing is weak	Increase your follow-through	173–74
Smash		
Not finding the ball well	Place yourself under the ball, as if you were catching it with your left hand	174–75
Mis-hitting the smash	Move your racquet to the ball slowly, then hit firmly but not too hard	175, 178
Not placing the ball accurately	The accuracy of the placement depends more on the racquet angle than the direction of the swing	178
No power on the smash	Approach the ball with the edge of the racquet, as if hammering the ball, then turn the racquet when you hit	174
Losing balance on the smash	Use the scissors kick when having to smash while leaning back	178
Hitting the legs with the racquet	As with the serve, bring the racquet down and across your front into the left hand	176, 177
Having trouble timing the smash	Raise your racquet slowly with the non-playing hand, while positioning yourself under the ball	175, 178
Not knowing whether to hit the smash forward or down	Always hit the smash down, and control the height and distance of your shot by opening or closing the racquet face	178

General Rules
and Competition

RULES

Tennis is governed by an international set of rules laid down by the International Tennis Federation and adopted by the U.S. Tennis Association (USTA).

Called *Rules of Tennis and Cases and Decisions*, these rules, together with the Code (the rules for unofficiated matches), cover every aspect of the game of tennis, from size and make of courts, tennis balls, and racquets, to scoring, competition, and correct behavior.

The *Rules of Tennis and Cases and Decisions* have been extended with USTA comments that clarify them to a far-reaching extent. Complete copies of these Rules and the Code can be purchased from the USTA, 70 West Red Oak Lane, White Plains, NY 10604; 914-696-7000; www.usta.com.

Some of these rules have been covered in earlier chapters in a simplified manner. Here we'll deal with additional general aspects of the rules.

The server shall not serve until the receiver is ready, whether it is a first or a second serve. If the receiver attempts to return the serve, he shall be deemed ready. Otherwise, he should make no attempt to return the serve while raising the hand to indicate that he wasn't ready, a "let" will be played, repeating the same serve.

A "let" can be called for a hindrance in making a shot, outside the player's control, but not the result of a permanent fixture of the court. For example, if a ball from an adjacent court comes into your court while the ball is in play, a "let" is called and the whole point is replayed, with the server being allowed a first serve.

A player may toss the ball up to serve, then decide to catch the ball instead, directly or after bouncing on the ground. Unless he attempted to strike it, he can replay the serve.

Any ball touched by a player before it lands outside his court is deemed to have landed in. Many players catch the ball outside the court during friendly competition, calling it out, but in any argument, remember that the rule states that if it touches you before landing, it is good.

A ball touching a line is deemed to have landed in the court of which that line is a boundary. Any ball that you cannot call out with certainty should be regarded as good.

The Code determines further rulings on decisions not covered by the *Rules of Tennis and Cases and Decisions*. For example:

In the event a match is played without officials, each player calls balls on his side, but should be scrupulously honest and fair to his opponent. If he can't call it out, there is no maybe. It is good.

The calls should also be instantaneous. If you called it incorrectly and the ball you called out is good, there is no replay. You've lost the point.

The server should announce the score in points prior to serving each point. This is a tradition kept by good players since the beginning.

Obscenities and bad language—as well as abusing the ball or tennis equipment—are considered "unsportsmanlike" conduct. In officiated matches such infractions are penalized.

Making loud noises can be the basis for a "let" or a hindrance, and should be avoided.

If you become a serious player, ready to compete, realize that there are innumerable situations not covered here that you may need to resolve quickly. Knowing the answer in advance is the best solution to avoiding problems in your matches that can result in an impaired performance. Go to www.usta.com and click on the "Rules/Officials" link, then on the "Rules of Tennis" and "The Code" links.

COMPETITION

The USTA is an exceedingly well-managed organization, dedicated to controlling, promoting, and developing all aspects of the game in the United States.

The USTA has approximately 675,000 members distributed over seventeen Sectional Tennis Associations, some of which comprise several states. Each section is a separate tennis organization, divided into districts, each with its own representatives and affiliated tennis facilities.

As an example, one of the USTA sections, the Florida Tennis Association (FTA), has over 750 affiliated tennis facilities in its sixteen districts. The FTA has a year-long calendar of tournaments in all age categories, plus major tournaments involving top professionals as well, including the Nasdaq Masters in Miami (which brings almost every pro in the game to Florida). Altogether, about 800 sanctioned tournaments are played in Florida each year.

Age categories in tournaments are 10 and under, 12, 14, 16, and 18 for boys and girls. For adults, the categories are Open Division, 25 and over, 30, 35, 40, 45, 50, 55, 60, 65, 70, 75, 80, and 85. There are also some special doubles divisions, like husband and wife, father and daughter, father and son, mother and daughter, mother and son, etc.

Several tournaments, including the USTA League, use a special rating system, the National Tennis Rating Program (NTRP) to classify and separate players according to their level. The USTA Leagues are team competitions and have regional, sectional, and national play-offs.

Senior tennis is extremely popular, not only at the local, state, and national level, but around the world as well. There are international tournaments in age categories above 35, 45, 50, and older. The USTA is increasingly associating some of this competition with the most serious tournaments. Where years ago pro players were washed up, competitively speaking, in their early thirties, today you see former world champions in their forties and fifties playing for prize money in front of enthusiastic crowds.

Each section publishes its own yearbook, in which every affiliated tennis facility is listed, with contact information if available, a complete schedule of tournaments, leagues, rankings, offices, and officials to contact, and a host of services such as recreational tennis programs, USTA school programs, teacher training workshops, programs for the disabled, and video and film libraries.

The following list shows where you can order your section's yearbook.

1. New England, 110 Turnpike Road, Westborough, MA 01581; 508-366-3450; fax: 508-366-5805
2. Eastern, 550 Mamaroneck Avenue, Suite 209, Harrison, NY 10528; 914-698-0414; fax: 914-698-2471
3. Middle States, P.O. Box 987, 1288 Valley Forge Road, Suite 74, Valley Forge, PA 19482-0987; 610-935-5000; fax: 610-935-5484
4. Mid-Atlantic, 7926 Jones Branch Dr., Suite 120, McLean, VA 22102; 703-556-6120, 800-532-8782; fax: 703-556-6175
5. Southern, Spalding Woods Office Park, 3850 Holcomb Bridge Road, Suite 305, Norcross, GA 30092; 770-368-8200; fax: 770-368-9091
6. Florida, 1 Deuce Court, Suite 100, Daytona Beach, FL 32124; 386-671-8949; fax: 386-671-8948
7. Caribbean, P.O. Box 40439, San Juan, PR 00940-0439; 787-726-8782; fax: 787-982-7783
8. Midwest, 8720 Castle Creek Parkway, Suite 329, Indianapolis, IN 46250; 317-577-5130; fax: 317-577-5131
9. Northern, 1001 West 98th Street, Suite 101, Bloomington, MN 55431; 952-887-5001; fax: 952-887-5061
10. Missouri Valley, 8676 West 96th Street, Suite 100, Overland Park, KS 66212; 913-322-4800; fax: 913-322-4800
11. Texas, 8105 Exchange, Austin, TX 78754; 512-443-1334; fax: 512-443-4748
12. Southwest, 2720 East Thomas Road, Suite B170, Phoenix, AZ 85016; 602-956-6855; fax: 602-956-0527
13. Intermountain, 1201 South Parker Road, #200, Denver, CO 80231; 303-695-4117; fax: 303-695-6518
14. Pacific Northwest, 4840 SW Western Avenue, Suite 300, Beaverton, OR 97005-3430; 503-520-1877; fax: 503-520-0133
15. Northern California, 1350 South Loop Road, Suite 100, Alameda, CA 94502-7081; 510-748-7373; fax: 510-748-7377
16. Southern California, P.O. Box 240015, Los Angeles, CA 90024-9115; 310-208-3838; fax: 310-824-7691
17. Hawaii, 1500 South Beretania Street, Suite 300, Honolulu, HI 96826; 808-955-6696; fax: 808-955-8363

Another publication you might want is the USTA Tennis Yearbook. This is a marvelous documentation of the complex role of the USTA, as well as a historical record of major championships and events. It also lists all its offices, officers, committees, representatives, rankings, champions, the season's results (both professional and amateur), awards, prize money, official rules, constitution and bylaws, tournament regulations, and much more.

index

Numbers in **bold** refer to pages with illustrations.

praise for the Wegner Method

"Oscar is a great coach. He makes the most advanced techniques of the game very simple and clear, and he has helped me regain my strokes and my feel for the game."

—**Bjorn Borg**, five-time Wimbledon champion and six-time French Open champion

"Wegner strips instruction of all those accepted phrases and directions that only clutter your mind and confuse. I think you will find it worthwhile to dump the past and join Oscar in your tennis future. In listening to him, I've unlearned a few things myself that I long considered gospel."

—**Bud Collins**, *Boston Globe*/NBC-TV tennis commentator

"Through his tips on ESPN International, Oscar has helped many of today's young pros and has been key in revolutionizing and simplifying tennis instruction around the world."

—**Martin Mulligan**, 1962 Wimbledon finalist and 1967 #3 ranked player in the world

"Oscar has dedicated his life to tennis, demonstrating the same passion for teaching the game as he had for competing. He's been at the forefront of research, molding the future of tennis [coaching]."

—**Guillermo Salatino**, FoxSports Latin America, founder and vice president of the International Tennis Writers' Association

"When my children were very young and just starting to play tennis, Oscar gave them drills that were fun, so that they wanted to play more and were motivated to play better. They looked forward to working with him and enjoyed the consistent improvements that result from his teachings."

—**Vincent Spadea Sr.,** father of Vince, top pro; Luanne, three-time Orange Bowl Champion; and Diana, winner of a U.S. National Junior Championship

"Oscar enhanced not only my tennis but also my life beyond description. I became one of the top juniors in the south of Brazil and went to college in the U.S. on a full tennis scholarship, where I achieved great results. A large number of other young players from my area—all of them somehow touched by the magic wand of Oscar Wegner's knowledge—followed the same path, playing college tennis in the U.S. on scholarships."

—Fernando Canziani Pereira,
marketing director and college professor

"Oscar has broken the mold used in understanding the modern tennis stroke. In working with him and watching super-slow-motion sequences of the top pros, I have seen the genius of Oscar's analysis of their dynamics and technique. He has translated this into an effective teaching methodology that is easy and fun to learn."

—Andy Rosenberg, director for NBC Sports
Wimbledon and the French Open

"With the application of Oscar's method, we definitely revolutionized tennis in the state of Santa Catarina, now a tennis powerhouse in Brazil. The results: the current top female player in the country, Nanda Alves, and nothing less than the sparkle that ignited Gustavo 'Guga' Kuerten, whose game was developed by Oscar and me until Kuerten turned 14."

—Carlos Alves, top Brazilian coach

"Oscar's techniques are incredible. Back in 1982 he was coaching with me in Germany and the students called him 'the American who taught tennis in two hours.' Over and over, he had total beginners rallying 40, 60 balls back and forth in just two hours of instruction. He also helped the Weiden Tennis Club enjoy an undefeated junior tennis team that year and send our main team to the Bundesliga."

—Jurgen Fassbender, former #1 player in Germany
and top-ten player in the world